920
CAR

T865600010779Z

Carruthers, Margaret W.

Pioneers of geology : discovering Earth's secrets

$14.96

DATE DUE	BORROWER'S NAME	ROOM NO.

920
CAR

T865600010779Z

Carruthers, Margaret W.

Pioneers of geology : discovering Earth's secrets

PIONEERS OF GEOLOGY

DISCOVERING EARTH'S SECRETS

BY MARGARET W. CARRUTHERS
AND SUSAN CLINTON

FRANKLIN WATTS
A Division of Scholastic Inc.
New York • Toronto • London • Aukland • Sydney
Mexico City • New Delhi • Hong Kong
Danbury, Connecticut

Photographs ©: Alfred-Wegener-Institute for Polar and Marine Research: 81 (J. Georgi), 68, 85; AP/Wide World Photos: 63; Corbis-Bettmann: cover background (Robert Garvey), 67, 82 (UPI), 36, 47, 62; Culver Pictures: 20, 30, 37, 44; International Stock Photo: 25 (Edmund Nagele); Liaison Agency, Inc.: 107 (Brad Markel); Malcolm Fife: 28; NASA: 116, 117; National Archives at College Park: 54 (photo no. 77-WB-31); Natural History Museum, London: 15, 21, 33, 89; Photo Researchers, NY: 56 (William Belknap, Jr.), 59 (Francois Gohier), 72 (John Cancalosi/Okapia), 106 (David Parker/SPL), 14 (SPL), 121 (NASA/SPL); Princeton University Libraries, Dept. of Geosciences: 93; Stone: cover bottom (Andrew Rafkind), 12 (Nancy Simmerman); The Art Archive: 34; TRIP Photo Library: 41 (Zoe Rogers); U.S. Geological Survey, Denver, CO: 49; Victor Englebert: cover top; Visuals Unlimited: cover center (Gary C. Will).

Interior design and page make-up by Vicki Fischman

Illustrations: Bob Italiano

Library of Congress Cataloging-in-Publication Data

Carruthers, Margaret W.
Pioneers of geology: discovering earth's secrets/Margaret Carruthers and Susan Clinton.
    p. cm.—(Lives in science)
Includes bibliographical references and index.
Summary: Profiles the work of six individuals who made important contributions to the field of geology: James Hutton, Charles Lyell, G.K. Gilbert, Alfred Wegener, Harry Hess, and Gene Shoemaker.
ISBN 0-531-11364-7
1.   Geologists—Biography—Juvenile literature. [1. Geologists.] I. Clinton, Susan. II. Title. III. Series.

QE21. C37 2001
550',92'2—dc21
[B]   00-027011

ACKNOWLEDGEMENTS

Foremost thanks go to the American Museum of Natural History in New York City. Its excellent natural history library and first-rate staff allowed us access to countless books and articles, including many original works. Additional resources were provided by the New York Public Library, the libraries of Columbia University and the Carnegie Institution of Washington, the Library of Congress, and the Bodleian Library of the University of Oxford, England.

This book benefited greatly from the biographical and historical works of John Playfair, Dennis Dean, Don McIntyre, Leonard Wilson, Stephen Pyne, Martin Schwarzbach, Ursula Marvin, H. W. Menard, Anthony Hallam, David Levy, and Don Wilhelms. Thanks also to George Hess, David Levy, John Maxwell, Walter Pitman, George Wetherill, Don Wilhelms, and Don Wise for their useful discussions, comments, and anecdotes.

Finally, I would like to thank those who made Earth and other planets come alive for me, most notably Jon Edwards at the Maryland Geological Survey, Bran Potter and Steve Shaver at the University of the South, and George McGill at the University of Massachusetts.

—Margaret W. Carruthers

CONTENTS

INTRODUCTION

This is a book about the lives and work of six geologists who made enormous contributions to our understanding of Earth. Geologists study Earth: its structure, its history, and the forces that continue to shape it. Geology is a relatively young science. For most of human history people relied on religious authorities to explain the physical world. Different cultures had different stories about Earth's origin and its features—land and sea; mountains and rivers. In the western world, the Bible was the most important source of ideas about Earth. Right up until the nineteenth century, people believed in an unchanging Earth that was about six thousand years old.

The scientific study of Earth began only about 250 years ago. Since then, this science has replaced the old idea of a static, unchanging Earth with a new understanding of this dynamic planet. Scientists now estimate that Earth accumulated from a cloud of gas and dust more than four and a half billion years ago.

Moreover, we now know that Earth's surface is always changing. The evidence is everywhere, but some of the changes are so ordinary that they can be difficult to see! Swollen streams wash away soil. Waves pound the shore, wearing away cliffsides and beaches. Plant roots and frozen ice crack rocks apart. Wind scours rock with dust and sand. Other changes are so immense and so slow that they are difficult to even imagine. Heat and pressure alter Earth from within. Mountains rise and then erode away. In fact, Earth's entire surface is mobile: it is divided into large slabs known as plates, which move about like icebergs, colliding into one another to produce mountains; grinding past each other to cause earthquakes, and pulling away from each other to form great rift valleys. Ocean floors solidify from molten rock that wells up at deep ocean rifts. This new ocean floor moves away from the rifts like a giant conveyor belt. After millions of years, it plunges back into Earth's interior, forming deep ocean trenches. Continents have formed, grown, come together as supercontinents, and then dispersed. All of these processes are slow, but they are ongoing.

Who were the first geologists? It's hard to say. The roots of Earth science go back thousands of years to when people consciously began using what they found on Earth to survive. By making stone tools, choosing the right soil for their crops, and mining minerals, such as gold, copper, and salt, people slowly began to understand rocks and minerals.

People couldn't help but observe and think about their environment. Numerous people throughout history noticed shells of marine creatures way up in the hills and mountains, far from any sea. Those living along great rivers like the Nile and the Ganges watched the rivers flood the land and wash sediments down to the sea. The Greeks experienced many earthquakes, observed that they changed the landscape, and made speculations about what caused them. Romans witnessed the eruption of Mt. Vesuvius in A.D. 79 and wondered what could have caused such a catastrophic event. Even if people couldn't come up with a reason why all of these phenomena occurred, they took the first step—they made careful observations.

In the seventeenth and eighteenth centuries, during the Enlightenment, or the Age of Reason, natural philosophers (there was no such word as scientist until the nineteenth century) really began to study and understand Earth. They collected and consolidated ob-

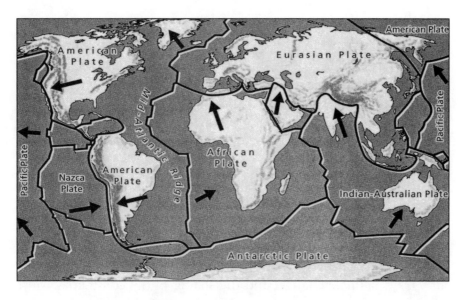

The theory of plate tectonics states that Earth's continents and ocean floors are part of huge slabs—or plates—of rock. These plates are moving—colliding, moving apart, and grinding past one another. These movements have created (and still are creating) many of the great features on Earth's surface, including faults, mountain chasms, rift valleys, deep trenches, and even the continents and ocean basins themselves.

servations into systems of knowledge. More importantly, they insisted on reasoning based on observation, rather than speculation based on faith, as the only reliable way to learn about Earth. Geology, the real *science* of Earth was born.

This use of observation and reasoning was basic to the work of **James Hutton** (1726–1797), a Scottish physician. Hutton was not the first geologist, but he is known as the first modern geologist. He reasoned that rocks and landscapes of the past formed the same way they do in the present—the present is the key to the past. This is now known as the principle of uniformitarianism and it is the cornerstone of geological science.

The English barrister **Charles Lyell** (1797–1875), through his books, articles, and lecture tours, popularized geology and promoted Hutton's approach to it. Lyell convinced scientists that uniformitarianism was the scientific way to study Earth. **G. K. Gilbert** (1843–1918) is often called the greatest American field geologist of all time. Working for the newly formed U.S. Geological Survey, Gilbert used his outstanding skills of observation and reasoning to understand Earth's crust by way of the American West—its mountains, canyons, ancient lakes, craters, earthquakes, rivers, and glaciers.

Alfred Wegener (1880–1930) was a German meteorologist and explorer. He pulled together information from many sciences—geology, geophysics, paleontology, biology, and climatology, to develop the theory of Continental Drift. This theory—that continents move around slowly on Earth's surface—could explain mountain chains, rift valleys, climate change, and the shapes of the continents. Most geologists did not accept Wegener's theory until thirty years after his death, when they were able to explore the ocean floor.

Harry Hess (1906–1969), a geologist and commander in the U.S. Navy, combined Wegener's evidence with new information about the seafloor to formulate the theory of seafloor spreading. This theory has now evolved into the theory of plate tectonics. And finally, **Gene Shoemaker** (1928–1997) of the U.S. Geological Survey, took geological exploration on to the next frontier: outer space. He studied Earth and then applied what he learned to understand our moon, and the other rocky planets and moons in our solar system.

Writing an entirely accurate history of a science is very difficult. It is relatively easy to find out when a scientist lived, where he or she traveled, and what he or she wrote about. It is a little more difficult to find out when something was invented and who invented it. It is even more difficult to find out when a place, or an object, or a natural phenomenon was first discovered and who discovered it. And it is almost impossible to figure out when an idea first crept into someone's mind, and whose mind it crept into first. Most ideas do not jump fully-formed into someone's head, but instead evolve through many minds over time.

None of these men worked independently; very few of their ideas were completely new or unique. Each worked with numerous collaborators: field companions, professional colleagues, teachers and students, friends and family. Each depended on the work of all the explorers, experimentors, inventors, and scientists who lived before. In addition, as for every person throughout history, the success of each man and his ideas was a result of his education, his place in society, the country he lived in, the technology and politics of his time, and to some extent chance, as well as his intellect and endless hours of hard work.

Why are no women featured in this book? Until very recently, geology was not a field in which women excelled. This is not because they weren't smart enough or strong enough, but because it just wasn't acceptable or even possible for most women to leave their homes, husbands, and children to go out into the countryside or wilderness to study rocks. Actually, there were women who made important contributions to geology: Mary Lyell and Else Wegener almost certainly contributed to their husbands' work; and William Buckland's wife, Mary Moreland Buckland, who was an accomplished naturalist herself, worked side-by-side with her husband in the field, and illustrated and edited his works into elegant masterpieces. There are no doubt many others whose work was never acknowledged and has since been lost. One notable exception is Florence Bascom (1862–1945), who became an expert on the geology of the Appalachians, and a professor to many successful women at Bryn Mawr College. Another very important figure was Inge Lehmann (1888–1993), a Danish seismologist. In the 1930s, she discovered that there is a solid inner core within Earth's liquid outer core. There are now women active in every field of geology. In the United States, more than one-third of geology students and about one-sixth of geology professors are women.

The rapid advances in geology that have changed people's image of Earth have also added vast amounts of data to the field and made the science more and more complex. The geologists we have pro-

Today, geologists carry out their research in extreme locations.
These two geologists are studying rock formations high on a ridge
in the Chugach Mountains of Alaska.

filed could all be described as physical geologists, who studied
Earth as a whole.

Many geologists today work in very specialized fields, such as
geophysics, mineralogy, geochemistry, paleontology, hydrology, and
petrology. Discoveries in all of these specialities still require a com-
bination of observation and imagination. Thousands of thinkers
have made geology what it is today. This book will introduce you to
some of them. We hope that you will come away understanding
some of the basic concepts in geology, how geologists think, how
they go about observing Earth and the other planets, and how their
ideas have developed over time.

"Carried Back in Time"

JAMES HUTTON AND UNCONFORMITY

In the summer of 1785, James Hutton, a Scottish gentleman, closed the door of his study behind him and set off hunting. A nobleman had invited Hutton to come along on a deer hunt in his forest at Glen Tilt in central Scotland, several days' ride north from Hutton's home in Edinburgh. The place is named for the River Tilt, which flows through the rocky, wooded foothills of the Grampian mountain range. Hutton gladly went along, but he was not hunting for deer; he was hunting for granite.

Granite is not hard to find in the Grampians. Granite masses underlie some of its peaks and granite boulders litter the Tilt bed. However, Hutton was hunting for a special kind of formation. He wanted to find places where the granite was in contact with the grey schist, the crystalline rock, that made up the rest of the mountains. He wanted to see what that contact looked like. What he expected and hoped to find were veins, jagged lines of granite, tracing their way through the grey schist.

In thirty years of observing and thinking about soil and rivers, rocks and landforms, Hutton had come to understand Earth in a new way, a way that completely contradicted the scientific teachings

James Hutton (1726–1797)

of his times. To Hutton, his chain of reasoning seemed so clear and so logical that it simply had to be true. Granite veins would be a key piece of evidence for his theory.

Instead of riding through the Glen after deer, Hutton walked the riverbanks with his eyes on the ground. He knew the geology of the region well enough to know that the contact between the granite and the grey schist had to be around there somewhere. Then he saw it. For a mile along the river, beautiful veins of red granite cut clearly across layers of the grey rock. Hutton enjoyed a moment of triumph. A friend wrote, "The guides who accompanied him were convinced that it must be nothing less than the discovery of a vein of silver or gold that would call forth such strong marks of joy and exultation."

What had Hutton proved? For a start, he could now show that granite is not a sedimentary rock. Sedimentary rock builds up as particles settle out of a body of water to form a thicker and thicker layer on the bottom. The pressure of material building up on top hardens the layers below. Some rocks, such as sandstone and limestone, form this way, but leading geologists of Hutton's time held that *all* rock was sedimentary. In thinking this, they followed the teachings of a famous German professor named Abraham Gottlob Werner.

Werner's school of thought was called "Neptunism." He taught that all rock layers on Earth had settled out of waters that once flooded the entire globe. The heaviest particles settled down first to form granite. This is why, according to Werner, granite formed the core of mountain ranges—it was the oldest, densest kind of rock on Earth.

Abraham Werner believed that great floods had once covered Earth. He thought that these floods had formed the geological features of the planet. His philosophy was called Neptunism, after the Roman god of the sea, Neptune.

Hutton disagreed. How could the Glen Tilt veins be sedimentary? The particles could not have fallen through a layer of solid rock. Clearly, the granite had flowed in, filling every crack and fissure. Although it was now solid, the granite must have been liquid when this happened.

Inside Earth, there had to be heat great enough to melt granite and propel it into layers of rock above. Mountain cores are made of granite, not because granite was laid down first, but because heat and pressure made the granite surge up under older rock. Granite was actually *younger* than the rocks above it. Granite was proof that there was a tremendous amount of heat within Earth. Hutton and his followers were called "Plutonists" because they believed that granite and other igneous rocks came from molten material within Earth.

These ideas were revolutionary, and Hutton went even further. Werner taught that Earth's surface was sculpted by a single event—a flood that covered the planet several thousand years ago. The flood gave Earth its permanent, final form. Werner knew about volcanoes and river erosion, but he didn't think these forces changed Earth in any important way. Processes that he could observe—volcanism and river erosion—were insignificant.

Hutton, on the other hand, wrote that the formation of Earth with its mountains, valleys, land masses, and oceans, didn't happen all at once. He argued that the planet was millions of years old, that it formed slowly, bit by bit, and that it is still forming and changing today. According to Hutton, the forces that everyone can see forming rocks and shaping the landscape today—the forces of rain, rivers, wind, volcanoes, and earthquakes—are the very same forces that formed the planet in the past.

Hutton's ideas were admired by his circle of friends, attacked by the Neptunists, and ignored by the rest of the world. In the eighteenth century, not many people knew anything about geology. Although a few schools taught practical courses in mining, none offered geology classes. Geology was a pursuit for gentlemen-scholars, men with the intelligence, the leisure, and the resources to follow their interests in a serious way.

THE YOUNG JAMES HUTTON

Born on June 3, 1726, Hutton was the only son of a well-to-do Edinburgh merchant. Unfortunately, his father, William, died when James was only three. His mother, Sarah, was left to raise James and his three sisters alone. The family staked their future on James. They had enough money to send him to high school and, at age fourteen, to Edinburgh University.

When his logic teacher described a chemistry experiment to illustrate a point, James was fascinated, not by the logic, but by the chemistry. From that day on, Hutton began to teach himself chemistry, doing his own experiments and reading everything he could find.

All of Hutton's friends knew how obsessed he was with chemistry, but for some reason they persuaded him, instead, to go into business. So after graduating in 1749, he went to work as an apprentice to a lawyer. Ideally, apprenticeship was on-the-job training; Hutton would learn about law while earning his keep copying documents. Instead, Hutton often amused his fellow apprentices with experiments when he should have been working. Bright, inventive, and absolutely bored by the law, Hutton must have been a nuisance in the office. The lawyer soon released him from his apprenticeship.

For someone interested in chemistry in the mid-1700s, medicine was the logical choice of professions. There was no medical school in Scotland, so Hutton went to Paris to study anatomy and then on to the University of Leyden, Holland, to finish his medical degree. After graduating, he spent a few months in London trying to figure out what to do with his life. Dr. Hutton realized that although he liked medicine, practicing wouldn't give him any time to experiment on his own. Fortunately, he had some alternatives.

In Edinburgh, Hutton and a friend, James Davie, had experimented with producing sal ammoniac from coal soot. Edinburgh was in the throes of the Industrial Revolution so there was plenty of coal soot and a great demand for sal ammoniac, which was useful in soldering metals. Hutton eagerly accepted when Davie offered him a partnership in his promising business.

Hutton's father had left him two small farms in Berwickshire, about forty miles southeast of Edinburgh. Rather than join Davie actively in the sal ammoniac business, he planned to use his inquisitive mind to experiment with agriculture. Hutton decided to run these farms according to the best methods available. Always thorough in his pursuits, Hutton spent several years learning innovative methods of plowing and crop rotation.

Traveling around England, on foot or on horseback, Hutton amused himself with the ground underfoot. In 1753 he wrote to a friend that he was "becoming very fond of studying the surface of the earth and was looking with anxious curiosity in to every pit, or ditch, or bed of a river that fell in his way." He became skilled at identifying minerals and began collecting rocks, "to illustrate the changes which fossil [rock] bodies have undergone." He observed weathered rocks being cracked and crumbled by roots, ice, and water. He saw rain-swollen streams washing away mud, sand, and gravel. He identified rock layers made of compressed mud, sand, or gravel.

Hutton's observations made him wonder about the previous lives of rocks. The hard mudstones, sandstones, and gravel conglomerates must once have been mud, sand, and gravel eroded out of even older rocks. How long had these processes been going on?

Hutton managed his farms in quiet, rural Berwickshire for fourteen years. Off and on, he made trips throughout Scotland and England, turning over questions in his mind. He wondered how layers of rock that should be lying flat got folded and turned on end, and why limestone deposits full of seashells cropped up far from any sea. During these years, Hutton's revolutionary theory of the Earth took shape.

HUTTON MOVES TO EDINBURGH

By 1767, managing the farms was no longer much of a challenge, so Hutton rented them out and moved, with his three unmarried sisters, to a house in Edinburgh. Edinburgh at this time was the center of the intellectual life of the Scottish Enlightenment, home to many brilliant people, such as philosopher David Hume, economist Adam Smith, inventor James Watt, and chemist Joseph Black. Hutton felt at home in this company.

For the first time, with no money worries, no farm to run, and three sisters to take care of him, Hutton had, ". . . the most enviable situation in which a man of science can be placed. He was in the midst of a literary society of men of first abilities, to all of whom he was peculiarly acceptable, as bringing along with him a vast fund of information and originality, combined with that gayety and animation which so rarely accompany the profounder attainments of science. Free from the interruption of professional avocations, he enjoyed the entire command of his own time, and had sufficient energy of mind to afford himself continual occupation."

Hutton did not live in grand style; he dressed simply and his manner was unpretentious. His friend and biographer John Playfair wrote, "It was always true of Dr. Hutton, that to an ordinary man he appeared to be an ordinary man, possessing a little more spirit and liveliness, perhaps, than it is usual to meet with." Hutton never married, although after his death, his friends discovered that he had an illegitimate son, also named James, and seven grandchildren in London.

On an ordinary day, Hutton spent his mornings in a study crammed with books, chemical apparatus, fossils, rocks, and minerals from all over the world. He eagerly read travel books, such as Captain James Cook's *Voyage to the Pacific* or Horace Benedict de Saussure's *Travels in the Alps*. In the afternoons, he performed chemistry experiments, studied his collections, or took long walks around Edinburgh, to places like Arthur's Seat and Salisbury Crags, where he could study the layers of sandstone and basalt. Once in a

Most of what we know about Hutton's theories come from the writings of John Playfair. He was Hutton's friend and biographer. Playfair was also a professor of natural philosophy at the University of Edinburgh.

while he worked as a geological consultant, advising engineers where to dig canals, or evaluating coal resources for the government. Hutton often spent the evenings dining and conversing with friends.

Hutton himself was lively and entertaining company, playful and good-humored. He was welcomed into the Philosophical Society, a group of well-educated gentlemen who met monthly to share accounts of their scientific work. These serious amateurs studied all kinds of subjects—weather patterns, chemical reactions, wine-making, agricultural advances. Hutton himself presented papers on botany and artillery as well as on geology. The Society gave Hutton an informed audience for his ideas.

HUTTON PRESENTS HIS THEORY

In 1783, King George III officially recognized the Philosophical Society, renaming it the Royal Society of Edinburgh. In honor of the group's new standing, Hutton agreed to present his "Theory of the Earth." He had discussed his ideas informally with his friends many times. Still, when the day came for the first lecture, Hutton was apparently so nervous that he got sick. Hutton's friend, Joseph Black, had to read the first half of his paper for him at the meeting of March 7, 1785. Hutton was well enough to read the second half the next month, on April 4, 1785.

Hutton combined his observations of the continuous erosion that broke rock into soil and washed soil into the sea with his observations of rocky cliffs that had obviously formed from particles of sand or shells of sea creatures. He thought that the *continuous*

This drawing shows two members of the Philosophical Society of Edinburgh. Hutton is shown on the left. The other person is Joseph Black. He was a chemist who first identified carbon dioxide as a gas and studied the effects of heat on liquids.

process of erosion was balanced by the *steady* formation of new rock layers under the sea. But exactly how did those new layers form? And how did rocks that formed under the ocean rise up out of it?

Hutton knew that this process was beyond human observation. It happened too slowly, in the unreachable depths of the sea. But he did think he could *reason* out the cause. Two forces could turn loose sediment into solid rock: water and heat. If water was responsible, then water must be able to dissolve the components of every solid rock. In Hutton's experience, there were many minerals that water could not dissolve. But heat, with the help of pressure from overlying rocks, could fuse together almost anything.

Heat was Hutton's answer. He had heard accounts of erupting volcanoes such as Laki in Iceland, and he was convinced by his own careful observations that some rocks must have once been molten: he *knew* that heat was an important factor. It could turn sand into sandstone, pebbles into conglomerate, and chalky earth into limestone. The expanding power of heat could raise continents out of the sea, breaking and folding them during the process. (How the continents stayed up, however, was another problem.)

Hutton's theory presented a continuously recycling Earth. As water eroded land away, heat formed and uplifted new land. These processes repeated indefinitely, with new landforms and new oceans constantly replacing one another on Earth's surface. There was no way of telling how many times this had already happened; no way of knowing how old Earth was or predicting when it might end. As Hutton concluded, "we find no vestige of a beginning, no prospect of an end."

This last sentence is the one critics fastened on. They thought that Hutton meant there really was no beginning to Earth history and that there would be no end. This was completely against the teachings of the Bible and they accused him of atheism. Hutton didn't actually mean that there was no beginning or end to Earth. He just meant that there was no *evidence* for a beginning and no sign of an end anytime soon. He purposely excluded the Bible stories from his theory. Hutton firmly put Biblical events outside the scope of science.

Hutton was not an atheist; he was a Deist. Deists followed no formal religion; they found God through nature. To a Deist, studying the natural world was the best way of coming to know God's wisdom and power. These religious beliefs led Hutton to make two assumptions that influenced his work: first, that the natural world expresses God's perfect design. Second, God designed Earth to provide a home for mankind. Hutton wrote, "He [man] alone is capable of knowing the nature of this world . . . and he alone can make the knowledge of this system a source of pleasure and the means of happiness."

Learning about Earth was certainly a source of delight and religious fulfillment to Hutton; however, no scientist today could base his work on Hutton's religious assumptions. Neither the idea that Earth is in a perfect and permanent form, nor the idea that the planet exists for man's benefit, is acceptable as a scientific principle. But Hutton's beliefs did allow him to approach Earth history in a new way. Hutton let Earth explain itself. He insisted on accurate observation and *reason* as the key to scientific understanding. He considered rocks, not the Bible, to be "God's Books;" an informed mind could read Earth's history in them.

In order to interpret rocks, Hutton developed an extremely useful assumption: "the supposition that the operations of nature are equable and steady." This means that the processes we see operating now have operated in the same way everywhere, throughout time. No matter how confusing or disordered Earth appears, the ordinary workings of nature can explain it, if only we could understand them well enough. His work established the study of Earth's history as a *science*.

Hutton had been very nervous about presenting his revolutionary ideas, but he needn't have worried. His theory aroused very little interest. His friend John Playfair wrote about this disappointing lack of reaction, "It might have been expected, when a work of so much originality . . . was given to the world . . . that men of science would have been everywhere eager to decide concerning its real value. Yet the truth is, that it drew their attention very slowly, so that several years elapsed before any one shewed [sic] himself publicly concerned about it, either as an enemy or a friend."

Playfair blamed this indifference on the numerous speculative scientific theories that had wearied readers. At the same time, revolutions and political upheavals absorbed men's attention in England and abroad. The United States had just won independence from Great Britain in 1783. French political discontent would boil over in the French Revolution in 1789. In the British Isles there was a mounting fear of new and godless ideas.

But Playfair also had to admit that Hutton's writing was at least partly to blame for the lack of reaction; "It was proposed too briefly, and with too little detail of facts, for a system which involved so much that was new, and opposite to the opinions generally received." When Hutton talked, his love of his subject, his depth of knowledge, and his generous eagerness to explain his ideas shone through. But his writing was stiff, obscure, and hard to follow.

HUTTON SEARCHES FOR PROOF

Hutton was not particularly concerned with being ignored. He continued searching for proofs that Earth was an ancient planet and that it was forming slowly and continuously. In 1787, on the Isle of Arran, a rocky little island off the west coast of Scotland, Hutton discovered another formation he had been looking for. Walking along the north shore of the island, he found layers of gray schist jutting out of the land at about forty-five degrees. The upturned end of the schist layer looked as if it had been sheared off. On top of it lay a flat bed of red sandstone.

Hutton knew immediately that this formation was powerful evidence that Earth was very old. The two rock types must have formed millions of years apart from each other. This type of rock formation is now called an *unconformity*.

Hutton found evidence for his theory after studying rock formations on the Isle of Arran, an island off the coast of Scotland. This photograph shows the upturned layers of schist. This rugged island covers 165 square miles (427 sq km).

The processes that formed the rock unfolded before him in his mind. The gray schist had begun underwater as a flat layer of mud and sand. After years of being buried and heated, it turned into hard, solid schist. Some other force then pushed the schist up on end, leaving it exposed to the wind and rain. Erosion slowly planed the jagged layers smooth. Only then did the ocean flood the land once again and deposit a layer of sand on top of the schist. Hutton knew that this process must have taken millions and millions of years. Geologists now estimate that more than one hundred million years lapsed between the formation of the schist and the deposition of the sandstone.

The next year, along the west coast at Siccar Point near his old home in Berwickshire, Hutton and Playfair discovered another outcrop of the same unconformity, where a horizontal bed of sandstone lay over layers of schist turned up on end. Playfair was deeply moved by the sight and even more impressed with his friend. He wrote, "We felt ourselves necessarily carried back to the time when the schistus on which we stood was yet at the bottom of the sea . . . An epocha still more remote presented itself, when even the most ancient of these rocks, instead of standing upright in vertical beds, lay in horizontal planes at the bottom of the sea, and was not yet disturbed by the immeasurable force which has burst asunder the solid pavement of the globe. The mind seemed to grow giddy by looking so far into the abyss of time; and while we listened with earnestness and admiration to the philosopher who was now unfolding to us the order and series of these wonderful events, we became sensible how much farther reason may sometimes go than imagination can venture to follow." This formation that outcrops on Arran and at Siccar Point is still known as Hutton's Unconformity.

Hutton's friends urged him to write a fuller version of his theory. They knew that he had gathered much more evidence to support his ideas, and they also knew that very few people would ever read the account from the meeting of the Royal Society of Edinburgh. If he didn't write it down, it could be lost forever.

At this time, Richard Kirwan, a very well-known scholar and teacher, published an outright attack on Hutton's theory. This was the incentive Hutton needed: immediately after reading Kirwan's attack, Hutton started on his book. Playfair recalled, "The reason he gave was, that Mr. Kirwan had in so many instances completely mistaken, both the facts, and the reasonings in the Theory, that he saw the necessity of laying before the world a more ample explanation of them."

In the summer of 1793, when he was sixty-six years old, Hutton began to have serious problems with his kidneys. He had to undergo painful and dangerous surgery. During a long, slow recovery, when he couldn't do much fieldwork, Hutton wrote.

In 1795 Hutton published a hefty two-volume *Theory of the Earth, with Proofs and Illustrations*. He continued to write a third volume, but the manuscript was lost after his death and it was not published until 1899, one hundred years later. Hutton never fully recovered from his kidney ailment. Another bout of the illness left him very weak, but he continued to read and study, entertain his friends with conversation, and even start a new book on agriculture.

THE END OF JAMES HUTTON'S LIFE

In the winter of 1796, Hutton grew weaker, thinner, and sicker. On Saturday, March 26, 1797, he was in pain, but nonetheless he began jotting down ideas about a new way of naming minerals. That evening he began to shiver. He sent for his doctor, but just as the doctor arrived, Hutton reached out a hand to him and died.

On January 10, 1803, John Playfair presented a biographical sketch of his admired friend to the Royal Society of Edinburgh. Playfair praised Hutton's brilliance as an observer and thinker who had made an extremely important contribution to science: "With him, therefore, mineralogy was not a mere study of names and external characters . . . but it was a sublime and important branch of physical science, which had for its object to unfold the connection between the past, the present, and the future conditions of the globe."

This devoted friend also made sure that Hutton's contribution would never be forgotten. In 1802 he published *Illustrations of the Huttonian Theory of the Earth*. Whereas few readers had struggled through Hutton's book, many learned about Hutton's theory in Playfair's clear and readable account. The book made a great impression on one reader in particular, a British gentleman-scientist named Charles Lyell. Lyell would expand Hutton's ideas and win worldwide acceptance for the new science of geology.

Hutton's gravestone is a testimony to his importance
to the science of geology.

Meanwhile, long after his death, Hutton's grave in Edinburgh's Grayfriar's cemetery was marked with a new stone; the stone reads, "The Founder of Modern Geology."

2 "THE PRESENT IS THE KEY TO THE PAST"

CHARLES LYELL AND THE THEORY OF UNIFORMITARIANISM

The Broadway Tabernacle in New York City was full to overflowing with a polite and eager crowd. The year was 1841. New Yorkers packed into the hall the see the latest visiting celebrity from England. Journalists scribbled descriptions into their notebooks. Later, pamphlets would reprint every word for the benefit of those who could not purchase tickets.

The crowd hushed as the star of the evening peered calmly at his notes. Then, in a low voice, he told the crowd about slow-moving glaciers huge enough to push the whole city ahead of them. He told about prehistoric mastodons and erupting volcanoes. He was not a good speaker, but the amazing things he had to say kept the crowd straining to hear. They wanted to catch every word about the latest discoveries in a new and fashionable field—geology. The lecturer was Charles Lyell, the most famous geologist of his—and perhaps of any—time.

By 1841 Charles Lyell had carved out a career for himself as geology's first international promoter and celebrity. Lyell knew all the right people, all the men of science in Great Britain, on the European Continent, and in the United States. Wherever he went—Switzerland, Italy, Denmark, the United States—scholars and

Charles Lyell (1797–1875)

scientists opened their studies to him and shared their research with him. Learned societies honored him. His three-volume book, *Principles of Geology*, went through twelve editions in his lifetime. His geology handbook for students went through six. Journalists followed him around on his 1845-46 U.S. tour. Sell-out crowds of thousands jammed in to hear him lecture in Boston and in New York.

Lyell became interested in geology at an exciting time. Everywhere he looked there were discoveries to be made. Throughout the Western world, able, well-educated men were turning their attention to geology. Lyell contributed some discoveries of his own, but his work is primarily valuable because he consolidated the rapid developments in the field.

Lyell's writings firmly changed geology from a battleground of sterile arguments into a respected science with sound methods and an agreed-upon body of knowledge. With his books and lectures, he kindled a widespread interest in the field that helped develop opportunities for other geologists. Between his lecturer's fees and his book royalties, he also made a sizable amount of money, more than enough to support both his scientific fieldwork and his gentleman's lifestyle.

YOUNG CHARLES LYELL

Charles Lyell was born on November 14, 1797 on his family's estate in Kinnordy, Scotland. His father was a prosperous landowner and as the first son, Charles would inherit the family's lands. Lyell's father did not work the farm himself; he rented the land to tenant farmers. The year after Charles was born, his father decided to move his family to livelier surroundings, so he rented an eighty-acre estate in southwest England called Bartley Lodge. Kinnordy was 535 miles (860 km) to the north—an eight-day coach trip that Lyell's father made yearly at harvest time.

The Lyells had a large family; Charles was the oldest of ten children (three boys and seven girls). Lyell's father himself had a strong interest in botany; he collected and identified plants, especially lichens and mosses. He encouraged his children to take an interest in the natural world.

At seven, Charles and his younger brother Tom began their formal education at a nearby boarding school. They spent holidays at home, free to roam Bartley's park and forest, watch the haymaking, and read in their father's well-stocked library. Even though their father required them to read and study while at home, it was a welcome break from lining up for stiff walks and memorizing Latin literature at school. For fun at school, Lyell recalled smashing flints to get the crystals inside, training mice to pull matchbox "chariots," and joining in chaotic evening pillow fights in the dormitory.

Although Lyell's father was very dissatisfied with the curriculum that emphasized Greek and Latin at the expense of science, he sent his boys on to the equivalent of high school at Midhurst. Older students bullied younger ones and Lyell wrote, "I felt for the first time that I had to fight my own way in a rough world." After two years at this school, Lyell's brother Tom left to join the Navy. As the second son, Tom would have to support himself. Charles Lyell stayed on at Midhurst, learning to write compositions in Latin and recite passages from memory.

Lyell still found more interesting things to learn about at home. It was in his father's library that he first came across the science that would change his life. Before picking up his father's copy of Robert Bakewell's *Introduction to Geology*, published in 1813, Lyell had never even heard of geology. Bakewell's book was fascinating because it described Earth as being very ancient, not a mere 6,000 years old as some theologians proclaimed.

In February of 1816, Lyell enrolled at Exeter College, Oxford, as a "gentleman commoner," an upper class student who paid more and got better food and living quarters than the poorer students. At the time, most of the students at Oxford were training to become ministers. Like Midhurst, the school offered a rigid classical education; the students read Greek and Latin, but there was no science major.

Many of the new developments in subjects such as chemistry were not taught at Oxford. And studying hard in any subject was unfashionable. It was fortunate that Lyell found a course that stimulated his interest. The course was in mineralogy. The lecturer, Reverend William Buckland, was a lively, genial, and unconventional man who entertained his students with his accounts of the great fossil reptile, *Megalosaurus*, and geological discoveries in England and Italy. He was so popular that his classes were always overflowing. On days that he didn't hold class out in the countryside with the landscape itself, he illustrated his points with a lecture room full of fossils he'd collected and colorful drawings and maps he and his friends had made.

Buckland would later write books trying to reconcile his religious beliefs with the fossil record. He was called the "last great diluvialist" because he believed that a series of global floods, like

William Buckland was a powerful instructor who used fossils as examples in his lectures. Buckland was a Diluvialist who believed that great floods had caused many animals and plants to become extinct.

Noah's flood in the Bible, could account for extinct species. Buckland and others, the Neptunists and Diluvialists, believed that Earth had gone through very violent changes, when land and sea shifted in global upheavals far greater than anything human beings would ever experience. These violent changes had caused whole populations of plants and animals to die out all at once, leaving layers of fossils. They also believed Earth had aged, cooled off, and calmed down from those wild, early times. Lyell admired Buckland and prized his friendship, although later he would come to disagree with Buckland's ideas and convince others (including Buckland) that the ideas were wrong.

Lyell's father was thrilled that his son had found something reasonable to occupy his mind. Charles Lyell began making his own geological observations. When they traveled up to Kinnordy, he visited fossil collectors and studied rock formations in mines and cliffs. When he went with his family to Europe, he spent time hiking alone in the Alps, walking on glaciers, observing rushing mountain torrents, and collecting fossils. While the family rode from place to place in a carriage, Charles Lyell walked, as much as forty miles (64 km)a day, he claimed, studying the land as he went.

Buckland made this drawing of the fossil remains of a giant Megatherium. This extinct beast, found in Pleistocene deposits in South America, was similar to a sloth.

LYELL JOINS THE GEOLOGICAL SOCIETY

In 1819, when he was only twenty-two years old, Lyell was elected a fellow of the Geological Society of London. This was a group of mostly wealthy amateurs who shared a serious interest in geology. Members were encouraged to present new facts and observations in papers at the monthly meetings. The Society was a private club; new members had to be nominated and voted in. Selection was an honor. Most of the members had the income to support their scientific studies and travels. Making money from scientific work was frowned upon because there was a notion that profiting from science would compromise the search for truth. There was also a fair amount of snobbery among the men who thought that most people who had to *work* to make a living weren't worth talking to.

After graduating from Oxford, Lyell went to London to study law. The Lyell family did have money, but with ten children to raise and a family income vulnerable to bad harvests in Scotland, they didn't have an unlimited amount. Charles would ultimately have to work for a living.

Lyell studied to be a barrister, a lawyer who defended clients in court. Barristers were considered gentlemen and did not drum up their own clients. They waited for lower-class attorneys to bring them business. For the first few years, a young barrister would spend more than he earned, since it cost money to travel with the circuit judges from town to town. Lyell kept at it, off and on, for seven years.

At Oxford, Lyell had begun to have problems with his eyes. Reading made them swollen and painful. He had to study with a wet towel around his head. Lyell was a good-looking man of medium height, but he walked stooped over, peering closely at what he wanted to see. Over the years his eyesight grew worse. Moreover, he was becoming more and more interested in geology, and in 1827, he gave up law for good.

In 1822 Lyell struck up a friendship with Gideon Mantell, a young surgeon who was studying Cretaceous fossils of reptiles,

After he graduated from Oxford University, Lyell became a barrister.
For seven years he worked as a lawyer who defended clients in courts.

birds, shells, and plants in southeastern England. One of Lyell's great gifts as a geologist was his ability to envision Earth as it must once have been. When Mantell took him to the quarry these fossils came from, he saw that the clays and sands were similar to the sediments laid down at the mouths of great rivers today. Instead of bones, shells, and crumbly rock, Lyell saw the rich, live ecosystem of an estuary or river delta that must have covered the English downs millions and millions of years before.

Diluvialists like Buckland would have said that these fossils were the remains of one catastrophic event—the Biblical flood. But from this day on, Lyell was sure they were wrong. The fossils and sediments had accumulated over many years, gradually, in the same slow, continuous way that they do today.

Lyell became friends with Gideon Mantell. Mantell's interest in fossils encouraged Lyell's interest in geology.

Collecting and classifying fossils was crucial to progress in geology in Lyell's time. An English canal surveyor named William Smith had recently developed a new way of dating rock strata by the fossils they contained. He recognized that different layers of rock held different sets of fossils; moreover, these characteristic fossils occurred in a regular sequence or succession of layers. Smith's method provided a new way of correlating strata in different parts of the country by their fossil contents. It didn't matter whether the rock was found on a weathered surface, elevated high in a mountain cliff, or buried deep in a quarry cut. Smith reasoned that rock layers containing the same kinds of fossils must have been deposited in the same period of time, when these particular creatures had been alive.

By 1815 Smith had produced a stratigraphic map of England—a map showing rock layers in different parts of the country. Other people could use these maps to predict where important layers of rock, such as coal or clay, lay underground. His work gave a new sense of excitement and purpose to work in geology.

For the next fifty years, Lyell collected and studied fossils wherever he went. Over time, he worked out his own method for figuring out the succession of strata. It was very logical: Lyell compared the fossil species to living species. In a particular rock layer, he compared the number of fossil species that were still alive on Earth to the number that were now extinct. He reasoned that the larger the percentage that were extinct, the older the rock.

Lyell used his method to sort rock formations into three geological periods. He was working on Tertiary formations—rock layers found just below the most recent sedimentary deposits. The topmost Tertiary strata he called Pliocene ("plio-" means "major"), because a major percentage of Pliocene fossils are remains of surviving species. Below the Pliocene are strata from the Miocene period ("mio-" means "minor"), with a minor percentage of surviving species. The deepest and oldest Tertiary strata he called Eocene ("eo-" means "dawn"). This period is the "dawn" of the recent; very few of its fossil species are alive today. Along with some additions, these divisions of geological time are still in use today.

In 1823 Lyell journeyed to Paris to see the collections at its Museum of Natural History and to meet some of the influential and brilliant French scientists. While there, he accompanied geologist Louis Constant Prevost on excursions to local quarries. Prevost had studied deposits where freshwater and saltwater shells occur in alternating layers. The accepted explanation was that the sea had repeatedly flooded over a freshwater lake in great cataclysms.

Prevost disagreed with the accepted explanation. He figured that an inlet had become sealed off from the sea and gradually become a freshwater lake. Periodically, in years of heavy rains, swollen rivers flowing into the lake had disturbed the old beds of marine shells, spreading them over the freshwater sediments on the lake bottom. So, as Prevost emphasized to Lyell, these shell beds could be explained by very ordinary, ongoing processes. This idea, of looking for explanations in present-day processes, would become the central principle of Lyell's work.

In 1824 Lyell started studying the geology of Scotland. He looked closely at the bed of a drained lake near the family estate in Kinnordy. He saw that it was made of soft, calcium carbonate rich marl with a thin, hard crust of crystalline limestone on top. These young deposits were exactly like some ancient deposits he had seen near Paris.

Lyell went on to investigate a similar lake nearby. This lake had not been drained, the water was shallow and he found that he could actually *see* the limestone crust form. He watched as the calcium carbonate precipitated from the milky water to form the thin crust on top of the marl. Here was a clear piece of evidence that modern deposits were still forming exactly as ancient ones had. Lyell put these findings into his first paper for the Geological Society in 1826.

LYELL SUPPORTS HUTTON'S THEORY

With his former teacher William Buckland, Lyell visited Glen Tilt to see the granite veins first discovered by James Hutton. Lyell knew Hutton's theory from reading John Playfair's book, *Illustrations of the Huttonian Theory of the Earth*. The more Lyell learned about geology the more he favored Hutton's view, of a uniformly recycling Earth, over the Neptunist's view of an Earth formed and reformed in sudden violent catastrophes. The Neptunist's view compressed Earth's history into a short period of drastic change, whereas Hutton's theory required vast amounts of time. Lyell's observations led him to agree with Hutton.

In addition to writing for the Geological Society, Lyell had also begun writing magazine articles for the *Quarterly Review*. The *Review* published long, thoughtful pieces on important topics. Writing one of these articles took months of work. In order to review a collection of papers published by the Geological Society, Lyell had to summarize the entire field of geology. His editor surprised him by paying him for this article. Another contributor to the *Review* complimented Lyell and Lyell remembered the compliment, word for word, "I have shewn more tact in rendering a scientific Article popular & intelligible to the uninitiated than any writer he could find in town."

Next, Lyell was asked to review a controversial book about volcanoes. The author, George Poulett Scrope, wrote that volcanic cones built up slowly as layers of lava from different eruptions spilled out and hardened. Scrope's view was attacked by catastrophists such as Buckland and the followers of Abraham Werner who believed (even though they'd never seen it happen) that volcanoes had been formed all at once, catastrophically, from huge bulges of molten rock.

In 1828 Lyell went to see for himself. He visited the extinct volcanoes in southern France. In Italy, he studied the lava beds of Mount Vesuvius and the buried city of Pompeii. In Sicily, Lyell rode up the sides of Mount Etna and marveled at the layers of lava exposed in the walls of a valley that cut through the mountain slope. He saw that Scrope was right. He also saw that Mt. Etna rested on a base of fossil filled strata. What amazed and excited Lyell was that the fossils in these rocks were those of living species. Etna must have formed, layer by layer, in relatively recent times.

Because he was not earning much money as a barrister, Charles Lyell began to think seriously of writing a book. But it couldn't be just any book. In England in the early 1800s, even science writing was looked down on. Making a living by writing, selling specimens, or curating collections, was for the lower classes.

Lyell wanted to bring scientific writing up to a gentlemanly status. He would write a book for the gentleman-philosopher. Lyell wanted to explain the principles that should guide the science of geology. In his opinion, most things done in the name of geology weren't really science; the geologists were not going about their

Lyell climbed down into Mount Vesuvius in Italy to examine the lava beds. In A.D. 79, Vesuvius had erupted and buried the cities of Herculaneum and Pompeii under layers and layers of ash.

work in a scientific way. He found it distressing that even his admired friend and teacher William Buckland was influenced more by religion than by his own observations and reasoning.

After leaving the law, Lyell got down to work. During 1829 and into 1830, he wrote and rewrote until he was satisfied with what turned out to be the first of three volumes of *The Principles of Geology*. The main idea in *Principles of Geology* is now called uniformitarianism. Lyell held that Earth's face has been shaped by the same processes that we see around us right now, operating at the same rate, over long, long stretches of time.

The principle of uniformity states that the only *scientific* way to understand the history of Earth is to observe the actual processes taking place right now; the present is the key to understanding the past. This method is also called actualism. There was never a single period of more violent volcanoes or universal flood; no global catastrophes; no wilder, younger planet. Just the constant operation of wind, water, and heat. The volcanoes, earthquakes, and floods of the past were no more powerful or more extensive than those in modern times.

Uniformitarianism wasn't new; it was James Hutton who had first promoted it forty-five years before. But whereas most scientists ignored Hutton, they listened to Lyell. The first volume of *Principles of Geology* sold out before Lyell finished writing the second volume. It was clear that writing would provide a more secure income (and a more interesting life) than the law ever would. And it seemed that writing would not compromise his gentlemanly status after all. (In fact, he became so popular that he was eventually knighted and then promoted to baronet).

The second volume of *Principles of Geology* came out in December 1831. In it, Lyell discussed organic life. Because he saw Earth as in a steady state of balance, Lyell thought of organic life in the same way. He knew that many creatures are extinct, and that many contemporary creatures did not seem to exist in former periods, but he believed the extinction and emergence of species was constant, random, and balanced. New species emerged at the same rate as others died out. There was no net change, no progress, no direction.

Other scientists were noting a progression in fossil life from simple to more complex creatures, but Lyell refused to accept the idea. If he couldn't observe evolution happening, he couldn't believe it. One of his friends and admirers, Charles Darwin, took Lyell's book along as inspiration on his voyages. Darwin's theory of natural selection and the evolution of species would challenge Lyell's work. Late in his life, Lyell changed his position and came to accept Darwin's ideas.

In 1831, Lyell proposed to Mary Horner, daughter of a well-known educational reformer and amateur geologist. On July 12, 1832, Charles Lyell and Mary Horner were married in Bonn, Germany. Whereas Lyell himself was reserved and preoccupied with his thoughts, Mary Lyell was gracious, charming, and patient. She traveled with Lyell, making sure he was comfortable, and waiting out his geological excursions in rented lodgings. Because of his poor eyesight, Lyell had to dictate his writings. Mary herself wrote his letters, while he paced back and forth. A friend described him dictating, "Sometimes flinging himself full length on two chairs, tracing a pattern with his finger on the floor, as some thoughtful or eloquent passage flowed from his lips."

During their wedding trip through Germany and their visit to the Lyell family in Scotland, Lyell wrote and revised the third volume of *Principles of Geology*. Lyell once described his methods of work to Mantell: "I am obliged to be very careful of myself, having never been strong like you nor capable of much mental exertion at a time. My only chance is by never missing a day if possible to make out a tolerable good aggregate amount of work in the year." With publication of the third volume in 1833, Lyell had firmly established himself as the foremost geologist of his time.

LYELL TRAVELS AND LEARNS

In 1841 Lyell was offered two thousand dollars to give a series of lectures in Boston. He was eager to go. Two thousand dollars for twelve lectures was three times the going rate in England. It was more than enough money to pay for him and his wife to travel around the United States for the year.

In the United States, Lyell traveled quickly from place to place, seeing as much as he could and pumping everyone for information. American geologists were flattered by his interest, but irritated by the way he soaked up their knowledge and turned it into articles. They nicknamed him "the Pump." Lyell was criticized for absorbing the work of others into his own without giving them enough credit. Even his long-term English friend Gideon Mantell resented the scanty acknowledgment he received in *Principles*. Mantell felt that Lyell was too wrapped up in geology to take much notice of other geologists. After one visit with Lyell, he wrote, "Lyell, as usual, was too absorbed in miocene, pliocene, plistocene &c., to care for any other 'scenes'."

While in the United States, Lyell spent some time at Niagara Falls estimating how fast the falls was eroding back upriver. He saw the coal fields of Pennsylvania; ripple marks in New Jersey sandstone; the Dismal Swamp of North Carolina; and the site of an earthquake along the Mississippi River in New Madrid, Missouri. He immediately incorporated much of what he saw into his lectures.

Even though he wasn't a very good speaker, Lyell's lectures were very popular. People were excited by the images of former worlds. They were impressed by his nine-foot-high drawing of Mount Etna and life-size drawing of a mastodon. He was so popular that when he went back to Boston in 1845, people were scalping tickets to his lectures. Lyell returned to the United States in 1845 and 1852.

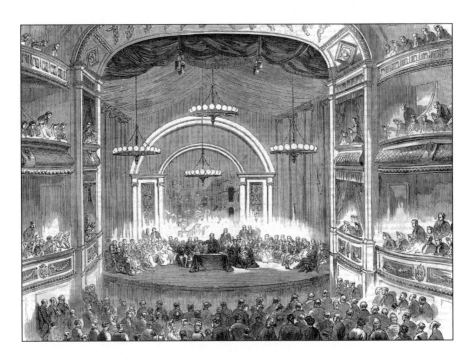

Wherever Lyell presented lectures, the auditoriums were packed. People were amazed at his stories of giant beasts that once roamed Earth.

Characteristically, he published two books about his time there, *Travels in North America, with Geological Observations* in 1845 and *A Second Visit to the United States of North America* in 1849.

Lyell once wrote to his friend Roderick Murchison that he had three pieces of advice for aspiring geologists: Travel, travel, travel! Throughout his life, Lyell followed his own advice. In 1834, he went to Sweden to look at evidence that the land was gradually rising out of the sea. Surveyor's marks made at sea level in the rocky coastal cliffs had risen 3 1/2 inches (9 cm) in fourteen years!

At Thun in Switzerland in 1835, the Lyells rowed about, dropping a five-hundred-foot (150 m) rope into the lake, measuring the depth in order to calculate the slope of the lake bed. He spent time on the Canary Islands; and went as far west as the Mississippi River in the United States. (Lyell never made it west of the Mississippi. The Rockies, the Badlands, the Grand Canyon, would wait for the next generation of American geologists.) In 1858, at sixty-one years old, he ascended Mount Etna in Italy once more.

He was always eager to read and hear about the discoveries of others, revising his own work in the light of new evidence. He wrote, "I sometimes think I am in danger of becoming perpetual editor to myself, rather than of starting anything new, except it be that my own work becomes new, & unlike its former self." He was especially interested in learning about places he was unable to visit. *Principles* included information about the deltas of the Nile in Egypt and the Ganges in India; it discussed volcanoes in the South American Andes, the Aleutian archipelago, and the Philippines.

Lyell worked at a time in the history of the science when it was still possible for one man to have a grasp of the whole field and to personally know almost everyone working in it. He managed to combine a tremendous amount of information in the *Principles*.

However, scientists disagreed about many topics and Lyell didn't always choose the correct side. For instance, some scientists, such as Louis Agassiz, were proposing that glaciers had once covered large areas of the earth. All across New England and elsewhere, Lyell saw huge boulders lying in fields far from any rocks of their kind. Geologists call these "erratics." Lyell claimed that icebergs or river ice had dropped erratics. Lecturing in New York, he said, "They [icebergs] grate along the bottom of the ocean, ploughing up mud and sand, with a force sufficiently easy to move a building like this, or even the whole city of New York before them!" Agassiz figured out that, not icebergs, but glaciers, grinding their way across the land, must have picked up boulders and then dropped them as they melted. Agassiz was right, but Lyell never accepted the idea of an Age of Glaciers.

Uniformitarianism, the method that Lyell promoted, of using present-day processes to decipher the past, remains the method of geology today. As he wrote, "History informs us that this method has always put geologists on the road that leads to truth, suggesting views which, although imperfect at first, have been found capable of improvement, until at last adopted by universal consent."

Although Lyell's uniformitarian view of a steady-state Earth gave the science of geology a sturdy working hypothesis, it was eventually "found capable of improvement." Scientists today believe that rare large-scale catastrophes, such as meteorite impacts, *have* had a role in shaping Earth. Unlike Lyell, they also believe that Earth *has* evolved through time, that it was a very different planet when it first formed more than four-and-a-half billion years ago.

Mary Lyell, who was much younger than her husband, died before him, on April 24, 1873. She had been a true companion to Lyell and made their home a social gathering place. Lyell survived her by two years, dying on February 22, 1875. As a final honor, he was buried in Westminster Abbey, along with English royalty and men such as Sir Isaac Newton, whose greatness was acknowledged in their own lifetimes.

Lyell, although too blind to read a geological map or observe a rock specimen in detail, had made geology popular and encouraged men to go about the science in a scientific way. He knew how im-

Although Lyell is shown reading, his eyesight was so bad that his wife Mary usually read to him. He died in 1875 and was buried in Westminster Abbey near other great scientists whose ideas have influenced our own times.

portant his work had been. He wrote, "For it must have appeared almost as improbable to the earlier geologists, that the laws of earthquakes should one day throw light on the origin of mountains, as it must to the first astronomers, that the fall of an apple should assist in explaining the motions of the moon."

"To Feel an Earthquake"

G. K. GILBERT AND THE STUDY OF LANDFORMS

On his 1876 expedition in Utah's Henry Mountains, G. K. Gilbert kept track of how many times each of his pack mules slipped and rolled downhill. In his notebook for November 13, 1876, he wrote, "Pangwich rolled over today into Curtis Creek. . . . Our little train of nine animals has attained to seven rolling scrapes." Gilbert took these small disasters in stride as he led his expedition along faint game trails towards Salt Lake City. He was coming in after a second field season in the Henrys with notebooks full of observations and ideas. Gilbert was a field geologist working for a United States government survey. To his geologist's eye, the Henry Mountains looked odd. Gilbert called them the Bubble Mountains; they bulged up from the plain as if they had been inflated.

These peaks, rising up to five thousand feet (1,500 m) above the surrounding plains, had dark centers encircled by tilted layers of sedimentary rock. Gilbert chipped off rock samples of the dark, igneous core rock and the sedimentary slopes. He mapped the contours of the mountains and measured the dip, the angle of the beds, of sedimentary strata. After his second field season there, Gilbert believed he understood how these odd mountains had formed; it was a process no one had ever described before.

G. K. Gilbert (1843–1918)

It would have been natural to assume that the Henrys were old volcanoes covered with layers of sediment that were deposited afterwards, on their slopes. But Gilbert saw that the dip of the sediments was too steep; no deposits could accumulate at that angle. The sedimentary rock had to be older than the igneous core rock; it must have lain in flat layers until the igneous rock pushed up under it.

Gilbert was also certain that the igneous cores were not actually old volcanoes. The rock did not look like hardened lava. Volcanic lava is extrusive: it pushes up and bursts through the surface. This rock was intrusive; it had pushed into rock above it, but never came to the surface. A century before, James Hutton had discovered that granite was an intrusive igneous rock, that it flowed into fissures and hardened to form veins in the rock layers above it. No one had ever suggested that magma could deform the rock it intruded.

The magma that welled up to form the Henrys had been hot enough to fuse and bake any rock it touched. It had enough force to arch layers above it, pushing them up into "bubbles." It formed dense, rounded mounds and never broke the surface to flow out as lava. Gilbert had to invent a new term for the rock boils: he called them "laccolites"; the term has since been slightly modified to "laccoliths." Over time, erosion wore away the covering sedimentary rock on the highest mountain tops to reveal the dark laccoliths underneath.

Gilbert published his report on the Henrys in 1879. At first, many geologists refused to believe that these mountains weren't sediment-covered volcanoes. There were still heated debates about laccoliths in the 1890s. Gilbert didn't worry about the contention. He was a soft-spoken, patient man with an aversion for politics and arguing. It didn't bother him that no one had ever described a formation like this before. He had seen it and had studied it carefully. He knew that his field research was sound and thorough; he was confident that his conclusions were correct. There was no need for him to fight in his defense when the facts themselves would eventually win out. Besides, there were too many discoveries just waiting for a geologist like Gilbert in the American West. Gilbert's explanation of the Henry Mountains is universally accepted by geologists today. And Gilbert himself is revered as one of the greatest American field geologists and a founder of geomorphology, the study of landforms.

YOUNG G. K. GILBERT

Grove Karl Gilbert was born in Rochester, New York, on May 6, 1843. His father was a portrait artist who taught his children drawing. Skill with a pencil would later become very useful to Grove Karl in his work; his field notebooks were always filled with drawings as well as measurements and descriptions. The Gilbert family was very close-knit. They nicknamed their house "The Nutshell," and spent their free time together composing poetry, playing card games, and taking turns reading aloud. Gilbert especially enjoyed solving the mathematical riddles and logic puzzles his father made up for them.

The Gilbert family never had much money to spare. When Gilbert was ready for college, at the age of fifteen, they scrimped to send him to the University of Rochester. At the university, he studied classics, foreign languages, and his favorite subjects, mathematics and engineering. He graduated in 1862, a year after the start of the Civil War. Many young men his age were joining the Union army, but Gilbert was not particularly hardy, and he did not want to go to war. He went to Michigan to try teaching instead. But the slim nineteen-year-old was no match for a room full of burly, rowdy high school students.

So Gilbert went back to Rochester and found a job at a scientific supply house called Cosmos Hall. Cosmos Hall supplied rock samples, fossils, artifacts, and scientific equipment to schools and museums. This business, now named the Ward Natural Science Establishment, is still thriving today. Gilbert's job was to sort and identify the specimens that company expeditions brought in. Sometimes he was allowed to go collecting himself.

An expedition to Cohoes Falls near Albany, New York, sparked Gilbert's interest in geology. He was assigned to help extract a mastodon skeleton from the cliffs along a stream. Gilbert noticed something puzzling about the streambed. It was pocked by deep, almost perfectly round holes filled with gravel. How had these holes formed?

While everyone else was reconstructing the mastodon, Gilbert studied the stream, trying to reconstruct the ancient riverbed in his mind. He figured out that the holes were gouged by gravel knocking against the bedrock. Once a small indentation formed, more gravel collected at that spot. Swirled around by the falls, the gravel would grind a bigger and bigger hole in the rock.

After five years at Cosmos Hall sorting specimens and artifacts from various expeditions, Gilbert was eager to venture out, see some of the world, and do some scientific work of his own. He applied to

Governor Rutherford B. Hayes of Ohio for a job on the Ohio State Geological Survey.

In the late 1860s, many states were commissioning geological surveys to evaluate their natural resources. Government officials wanted to know if the state had any deposits of coal, oil, or minerals, such as iron or gold, worth mining. The surveys also studied resources such as fertile soil, stands of timber, and navigable rivers. Gilbert did not have a degree in geology. Governor Hayes turned him down for a paid position. But the Survey's director, John Newberry, saw that Gilbert had a great natural curiosity, intelligence, persistence, and good nature, and he invited Gilbert to join as a volunteer assistant. It was a chance to learn field geology on the job.

Gilbert worked for Newberry from 1869 to 1871. From July to September, the Ohio geologists traveled along railroad and canal routes identifying rocks, gathering fossils, mapping geological formations, and studying the way ancient glaciers had shaped the land. Sometimes they surveyed on foot; sometimes they mapped from the windows of a moving train. From October to June, Gilbert wrote and illustrated reports, sorted their specimens, and helped prepare lecture material for Newberry's courses at Columbia University in New York.

GILBERT SURVEYS THE WEST

Newberry was impressed with Gilbert. In 1871 he thought it was time for Gilbert to see a different part of the country. Newberry recommended Gilbert for a position on a U.S. Government survey of the West.

Although prospectors had been streaming west since the Gold Rush of 1849, hoping to strike it rich, very little of the vast area west of the one hundredth meridian had ever been explored. (The one hundredth meridian forms the eastern boundary of the Texas Panhandle, continues through Oklahoma and Kansas, and cuts Nebraska, and the Dakotas nearly in half.) The spectacular Western landscape of towering mountains, rushing rivers punctuated by falls and rapids; and parched desert flatlands offered spectacular obstacles to travel, let alone systematic study. Nevertheless the press of settlers and the wealth of mineral resources prompted the U.S. Government to take stock of its Western territory.

Four separate surveys were operating in the West, under four different leaders: Clarence King, F. V. Hayden, Major John Wesley Powell, and Lieutenant George Wheeler. Each survey included its own geologists to study the rocks and landforms; topographers and surveyors to make maps; naturalists to report on the plant and animal life; photographers; guides; and laborers to carry all the gear, set up camp, and cook meals. All but Powell's survey traveled with a military escort to protect them from hostile Indian tribes.

In 1871 Gilbert became a geologist and surveyor for the Wheeler survey, assigned to work the dry, barren country where Nevada, California, and Arizona meet. Wheeler was an Army man taking orders from the War Department. He liked giving orders, seemed to revel in red tape, and did everything hastily. Scientific observations didn't interest him as much as noting the best routes for troops. Gilbert's first summer with the survey, Wheeler led them across Death Valley in Eastern California. Daytime temperatures hit 118°F (48°C); watering holes were far apart and hard to find. Some of the men died. Without the help of their Native American guides, the survey would have ended there.

That September, Wheeler decided to explore the southwestern end of the Grand Canyon. The entire Canyon had already been mapped by the Powell survey just two years before. But, Wheeler reasoned, Powell had ridden downstream. He would explore upstream. After thirty-three disastrous days of rowing against the current, pulling the boats up through rapids and carrying them past waterfalls, Wheeler and his men reached Diamond Creek. Along the way, all of the maps Gilbert had drawn and hundreds of photographic negatives, as well as much of their food, were lost when a boat capsized.

Exploring the wilderness often took Gilbert into remote locations. Here Gilbert (on the left) explores an area of Arizona with his Native American guides.

In spite of the danger, difficulty, and frustration of that first field season, Gilbert loved working in the wide open spaces of the West. He could see the strata of cliffs and mountains from miles away. He wrote, "The deep carving of the land which renders it so inhospitable to the traveler and the settler, is to the geologist a dissection which lays bare the very anatomy of the rocks."

Survey teams spent winters in Washington, D.C., where the leaders lobbied for more funding, while the scientists wrote up their reports. In Washington, Gilbert got to know Major Powell, the leader of a competing survey. Powell was conscientious and intelligent. He didn't let the loss of his right arm during the Civil War slow him down in the field. He took an interest in everything he saw: plants, rocks, fossils, river systems, Indian customs. He befriended the tribes in the areas he surveyed and studied their languages. Whereas Wheeler rushed his expeditions along, Powell allowed his men to spend the time they needed.

In 1875 Gilbert transferred to Powell's survey. Powell was active in Washington, D.C., urging consolidation of the four competing, and sometimes overlapping, surveys. Gilbert was content to leave politics to others as long as he was allowed to continue with his work. Powell had discovered the Henry Mountains; he sent Gilbert out to study them.

In 1879, after much squabbling and infighting, Congress united all the surveys under the Department of the Interior as the United States Geological Survey (USGS), with Clarence King as director and Powell as second-in-command. Gilbert was assigned to work in Utah. He was delighted. Several years before, he had noticed something about the Great Salt Lake that he wanted to go back and investigate.

The mountains rimming the Great Salt Lake had terraces, nearly level terraces very much like beaches, except that the first one was three hundred feet (90 m) above lake level and the second one was one thousand feet (300 m) above it. Gilbert realized that these terraces marked the shorelines of two ancient lakes, much deeper and much larger than Great Salt Lake. He named the largest and deepest, the one whose terrace lay one thousand feet high, Lake Bonneville, after the pioneer who first described the Great Salt Lake in 1833.

Gilbert got to work prying out rock samples, identifying fossils, and studying ripple marks in the terrace rock. He measured the thickness of the sediments to figure out how long the ancient lake had been there. He calculated its size and figured out why the water level dropped from its highest level, marked by the terrace at one thousand feet, down to three hundred feet, and then to the present level of the Great Salt Lake.

Lake Bonneville formed during the last Ice Age, as water filled the mountain-rimmed basin to a depth of one thousand feet. The ancient lake covered twenty thousand square miles (50,000 square km). Over long stretches of time, Lake Bonneville lapped at the mountains, cutting the beach terrace Gilbert had recognized. Then the lake overflowed. It began flowing north through Red Rock Pass. As water wore down the rocks in the pass, an immense torrent rushed through the pass and flooded the Snake River of Idaho. The lake level dropped and dropped until it stabilized as a shallower, smaller lake which Gilbert named Lake Provo. Lake Provo cut the second terrace into the mountains. As the climate became warmer, Lake Provo slowly dried up, leaving all the salt behind, in greater and greater concentrations. The present-day Great Salt Lake is all that remains of Lake Provo and Lake Bonneville.

Over a period of thousands of years, the waters of Lake Bonneville drained away and evaporated leaving a great salt desert. Gilbert studied the surface of the lake and took rock samples and fossils from the mountains in the background.

GILBERT DISCOVERS ISOSTASY
IN A LAKEBED

In making his measurements, Gilbert noticed something strange: the ancient lakebed was not level. It was lowest near the outer edges and bulged up about 110 feet (34 m) near the center. The lake bottom must have been flat when the sedimentary layers were deposited. It must have bowed up later, but why and how?

Many scientists at the time believed that Earth's crust was hard, brittle, and rigid. They calculated that it would crack or fault under pressure. To Gilbert, it seemed that in some cases Earth's crust acted more like a huge, immensely slow-acting blob of Silly Putty; it responded to pressure and very, very slowly bounced back. This concept, that Earth's crust adjusts to the loads put on it, is called isostasy.

The bulge in the center of Lake Bonneville is an example of isostasy. When Lake Bonneville flooded and drained into the Snake River, it relieved the crust of a tremendous weight of water. The crust bounced back just like a piece of wood, after being pushed down in water, pops back up to the surface. When Gilbert finally published *The Lake Bonneville Monograph* in 1890, it became an instant geology classic.

In 1881 John Wesley Powell took over as director of the USGS. Powell wanted Gilbert back in Washington. For the next ten years, Gilbert spent most of his time behind a desk instead of out in the field. Powell needed him to write reports and to supervise the projects of other geologists. Although he visited project sites and spent every vacation in the field, it wasn't enough. Gilbert missed the adventure of field work; he missed being able to delve into a problem the way he had at the Henry Mountains or at the Great Salt Lake.

During these years, the Gilbert family suffered a terrible loss when their only daughter, seven-year-old Betsy, died of diphtheria. Gilbert enjoyed a close companionship with both his sons, Archibald and Roy, throughout his life; however, he never got over the loss of his young daughter. Then, in 1883, all family members became ill from coal-gas, or carbon monoxide, poisoning. Gilbert's wife, Fannie, was affected the most. There was no way to reverse the harm that had been done to her. Fannie Gilbert slowly got weaker and sicker until she was a complete invalid. She died seventeen years later, in 1899.

During these sad years in Washington, the one bright, enormous landscape that Gilbert could focus on was the face of the moon. He spent many evenings peering through a telescope. He could see that the craters of the moon had different forms depending on their size. Small craters were bowl-shaped; large ones had flat floors, some with hills in the center. Craters were usually associated with volcanoes, but Gilbert suspected that lunar craters were created by objects smashing into the moon.

Because Gilbert never observed this happening, he needed a way to test his hypothesis. He worked up a batch of mud, threw spheres into it, and then compared the impact craters he created to those on the moon. Planetary geologists still study craters this way, but with high-speed projectiles and time-lapse photography. Gilbert was the first planetary geologist. Today, the most prestigious award in the field is the G. K. Gilbert Award.

Looking at the craters on the moon also made Gilbert wonder about strange craters on Earth. One of these was a crater four thousand feet (1200 m) across and 570 feet (170 m) deep known as Coon Butte in Arizona (it was later known as Barringer Crater, or Meteor Crater for the meteorites that are scattered around it). Most geologists thought that this crater was caused by a volcanic steam explosion. Gilbert was sure that it was actually a large impact crater that formed when a meteorite hit Earth. To prove it to himself, he needed to find "the buried star" in the crater. He never did.

Gilbert was an extremely careful scientist. His gut feeling was still that Coon Butte was an impact crater, but because he never found the evidence to support that idea, he could only conclude that it was volcanic. More than fifty years later, geologists investigat-

Gilbert examined Meteor Crater, which lies between the towns of Flagstaff and Winslow in Arizona. Geologists now know that the crater was formed about 50,000 years ago when a huge meteorite struck Earth.

ing Meteor Crater found evidence to prove that Gilbert's intuition was right after all.

In 1893 Gilbert gave up his USGS administrative duties in order to get back to the field. His first assignment was to study the difficult problem of water supply in the West. The summer drought and winter storms of 1885 to 1886 had ruined Western ranchers and homesteaders alike. It had also alerted the federal government to the need for large-scale irrigation projects. The USGS effort to map and plan for reservoirs was mired in political conflict. Resurveying to correct maps was tedious work for Gilbert. Nonetheless, he was delighted to be back out in the wilderness—he always considered a tent better than a desk.

Gilbert wrote to a friend, "Happiness is sitting under a tent with the walls uplifted, just after a brief shower, when most of the flies have quit lighting on the lobster-red wrists burnt during the morning ride. . . . It is rising at 4:30, while Jupiter is still palely visible but there is no longer any temptation to hunt for the comet . . . .and then sallying forth on the white horse Frank to study the limits of the alluvial veneering on the base-level mesas, measure the dips of rows of rusty nodules, sketch problematic buttes, and gather the houses of Ammonite, Scaphite, and Hamite. It is going to bed by early candle light in the midst of a grove of *Rhus tox*, hunting the double stars of Lyrae and Cygni among the branches of overhanging cottonwoods, moralizing on the development of character through the trying associations of camp life, congratulating yourself that you are not a pessimist, and finally dropping off to sleep."

In 1899 Gilbert joined twenty-four other scientists on an expedition to Alaska. His wife had recently died and Gilbert needed something to occupy his mind. Years before, in New York and Ohio, he had studied the landforms created by glaciers thousands of years ago. Now he would see them alive and in action. In two months, Gilbert studied forty glaciers. Some of them were growing, while others were retreating, with icebergs breaking off, calving, into the sea. He tried to understand how glaciers moved and what made them change shape over time. From shipboard, Gilbert mapped and photographed them to create a record for the future. He was a pioneer in the new field of glacial geology.

GILBERT GOES TO CALIFORNIA

In 1905 the USGS sent Gilbert to California's Sierra Mountains to study the effects of hydraulic mining. Miners, who began by panning gold nuggets out of the silt in streambeds, soon advanced to blasting away whole hillsides with powerful jets of water to wash down the gold. In thirty years of hydraulic mining, 1,300 million cubic yards (one billion cubic m) of Sierra slopes had been washed away. This sediment washed into the area's rivers, causing flooding and ruining agricultural land with debris. Over the next ten years, Gilbert studied the streams and measured the debris. He mapped the area and built his own huge flumes—water chutes—to conduct experiments on exactly how streams carry and deposit sediments.

Gilbert loved California and spent most of his later years there, settling in Berkeley. On April 18, 1906, Gilbert was awoken at 5:11 A.M. by a "tumult of motions and noises." His room was shaking back and forth, spilling water from the pitcher near his bed. He later said, "It was with unalloyed pleasure that I became aware that a vigorous earthquake was in progress." He had always thought that it should be the "natural and legitimate ambition of every properly constituted geologist to see a glacier, witness an eruption, and feel an earthquake."

Gilbert didn't panic during this quake or its many aftershocks. He observed that sometimes his room shook north-south, sometimes east-west. He clocked the time between tremors. This was (and still is) the strongest earthquake on record in northern California, although it didn't do too much harm in Berkeley. Across the bay, however, San Francisco was almost completely destroyed by the quake and the fire that followed.

Gilbert wondered why earthquakes occurred. Geologists knew that earthquakes were related to volcanoes. But this quake was nowhere near any volcano. Gilbert searched San Francisco for scarps, short cliffs formed when one section of land drops. He noted how roads and fences had been torn apart. This earthquake happened along a north-south fault or a deep crack in the earth. Pressure along the fault caused the rocks to shift. The west side moved north while the east side moved south. Gilbert wanted the city's architects and engineers to learn from this earthquake because he knew that it could happen again.

*On April 18, 1906, an earthquake struck San Francisco, California.
The earthquake snapped natural gas lines and overturned stoves and gas
lamps. Fires broke out all over the city. This photo shows people sitting on
Russian Hill watching the fires burn in the downtown area.*

This closer view of the raging fires shows how much damage was done.
The fires burned for three days. At least 3,000 people died and more than
250,000 people were left homeless.

G. K. GILBERT'S FINAL YEARS

One of his fellow voyagers on the Alaskan expedition in 1905 was naturalist John Muir, the founder of the Sierra Club. Although Gilbert didn't particularly like Muir himself, he did share Muir's love for the Western landscape and his desire to preserve it. Gilbert became an active member of Muir's Sierra Club.

On one of his Sierra Club outings, Gilbert met an enterprising botanist named Alice Eastwood. Eastwood headed the botany department at the California Academy of Sciences in San Francisco. She had managed to save thirteen hundred of the Academy's rarest plant specimens from destruction in the earthquake and fire of 1906. Following the quake, it took her six years to collect the California and Rocky Mountain plants she needed to rebuild the collection. The more they got to know each other, the more Gilbert and

Eastwood seemed to have in common. Their age difference—Eastwood was sixteen years younger—didn't seem to matter. They decided to marry in the summer of 1918. Unfortunately, Gilbert died that spring, on May 1, 1918, five days short of his seventy-fifth birthday.

G. K. Gilbert was one of the great field geologists; in addition to being thorough and meticulous he was intellectually daring and original. Geologists before him knew that forces of heat or erosion acted to shape landforms, but Gilbert's study of the Henry Mountains, the Sierra Mountains, ancient Lake Bonneville, even the moon, brought him to understand that Earth and its rocks are not simply acted upon. They affect the processes themselves. Under pressure, some rock layers break while others bulge and arch. Flowing water erodes away some rock layers, while more resistant rock seems to stand taller as the ground around it washes away. Over eons and eons of time, rock masses bend and fold, rise and sink, even bounce back from pressure. Landforms record an interaction between natural forces and rock masses. Gilbert's insight underlies the branch of geology now called geomorphology, the study of landforms.

In his Western travels, Gilbert noticed something he couldn't completely explain. The entire area from the Rockies to the Sierras was a series of parallel mountain ranges separated by valleys. Where a valley bordered a mountain, there would be fault lines, deep cracks separating the land mass of the valley from that of the mountain. Most geologists of his time would have guessed that the faults occurred when the mountains were pushed up above the level of the land around them. But when Gilbert studied the angle of the fault lines, he concluded that the opposite had happened. The valleys had dropped down.

Gilbert named this whole area the Basin Range. The land here was being stretched, pulled apart. The valleys were places where huge chunks had dropped to fill gaps. What was causing the land to spread and stretch here? Gilbert could not explain that. That explanation would come from a German meteorologist named Alfred Wegener. Wegener had published his theory of continental drift in 1915, three years before Gilbert's death, but it would be decades before geologists would accept his ideas. Gilbert had already noted one of the effects of continental drift; geologists still refer to that area of the West as the Basin and Range Province.

4 "A Geological Jigsaw Puzzle"

ALFRED WEGENER AND THE THEORY OF CONTINENTAL DRIFT

In 1906, twenty-five-year-old Alfred Wegener began his first winter on the bitterly cold northeast coast of Greenland. He was a meteorologist studying the polar atmosphere on a scientific expedition. Greenland's unforgiving climate had discouraged exploration; the area where Wegener was working had never even been mapped. He and the other expedition members lived in a little "winter house" and made their research trips on dogsleds. Every trip required care and planning; there was no margin for error. On one trip, Ludvig Mylius-Erichsen, the leader of the expedition, along with two other men, ran out of food. All three of them died before they could make it back to the base camp.

All that winter and the one that followed, Wegener had many chances to watch icebergs jostle against one another along the coast. Maybe these huge, floating masses first gave him the idea. Maybe he thought of it later while he was glancing over a map of the world. It is certain that by 1910, Wegener had set himself a scientific problem to solve. He mentioned it in a letter to his fiance, "Doesn't the east coast of South America fit exactly against the west coast of Africa, as if they had once been joined? . . . This is an idea I'll have to pursue."

Alfred Wegener (1880–1930)

Wegener did pursue it, gathering all the information he could find about rock formations; the distribution of fossil plants and animals; and climates of past eras. Wegener was neither a geologist nor a paleontologist, but he searched through both fields looking for information.

By 1912, Wegener had an answer to the question; however, it was an answer that almost no one was ready to hear. He proposed that continents were not fixed in permanent locations. They moved. Just like massive icebergs, the continents slowly, slowly drifted across Earth's surface. The contours of South America and Africa fit together like jigsaw pieces because at one time they had been parts of one large continent. At some point in the distant past, this landmass broke apart. In fact, he proposed, the pieces are still moving.

In 1915, Wegener explained his ideas in a book, *Die Entstehung der Kontinente und Ozeane* (*The Origin of Continents and Oceans*). We-

Initially, Wegner's main interest was polar meterology. He may have gotten the idea of drifting continents while watching icebergs drifting off the coast of Greenland.

gener's theory could explain so many observations from so many different fields, but he couldn't explain *how* the continents move. What force could possibly propel them? Continental drift caused a scientific furor, but without an answer to this question, most scientists dismissed the theory as a fantasy. New data that would support his theory would not be available for another forty years. By the time Wegener was hailed as the Father of Continental Drift, he was dead and even his grave marker was buried more than twelve meters deep under the featureless Greenland ice.

YOUNG ALFRED LOTHAR WEGENER

Alfred Lothar Wegener was born in Berlin, Germany, on November 1, 1880. His father, Richard Wegener, was a well-educated man, with a Ph.D. in theology and classical languages. Richard Wegener did some preaching, taught secondary school classes, and directed an orphanage for boys. He and his wife, Anna, had five children; however, two of their children died very young. Alfred was their youngest; he had an older brother, Kurt, and an older sister, Tony.

Details about Alfred's childhood are sparse. During the school year, the family lived in Berlin. They spent their summers in a northern German village called Zechlinerhutte where Alfred and Kurt were free to roam the countryside. As he grew up, Alfred wanted to become an explorer and he often dreamed of leading polar expeditions.

When it came time for Alfred to go to college, he did not follow his father into theology. Natural science interested him. He also did not follow his father's strict principles of conduct, at least during a summer semester at the University of Heidelberg. In July 1900, the local police fined him for parading down the street at 3 A.M., wearing only a sheet and "shouting loudly in an unseemly manner."

After a required year of military service from 1901 to 1902, Wegener went to the University of Berlin to study astronomy. For his doctoral dissertation, Wegener tackled a very technical, mathematical project. He recalculated a thirteenth-century set of tables for figuring out the positions of the sun, moon, and planets. Wegener earned his doctorate in 1904. But when it came time to look for a position for himself, neither astronomy nor mathematics attracted Wegener. He told a friend, "In astronomy everything has essentially been done. Only an unusual talent for mathematics together with specialized installations at observatories can lead to new discoveries; and besides, astronomy offers no opportunity for physical activity."

Meteorology, the study of the atmosphere, weather, and climate, offered Wegener more exciting possibilities. New developments in communications, such as the telegraph, the radio, and the trans-Atlantic cable, made it possible to track storms and forecast their approach. Wegener and his brother Kurt began working at the Royal Prussian Aeronautical Observatory near Berlin. They loaded kites and balloons with instruments and sent them up to gather data in the upper atmosphere. Sometimes, they went up in balloons themselves. In 1906 Alfred and Kurt Wegener made a balloon journey from central Germany to northern Denmark and back to Germany again. They stayed in the air for fifty-two hours, setting a new world endurance record.

Wegener's work drew the attention of Ludvig Mylius-Erichsen who invited him to continue his experiments on a scientific expedition to Greenland in 1906. Mylius-Erichsen himself did not survive the expedition, but Wegener came home after two years, having realized his dream to become an Arctic explorer. He brought back the first studies ever made of the polar atmosphere.

In 1908 he accepted an appointment to teach courses in astronomy, meteorology, and navigation at the University of Marburg. A lecturer's income was small and unreliable. Wegener received no regular salary from the University until 1915. Before then, individual students paid him for the courses they chose to take. But since Marburg had no official department of meteorology, the number of students studying Wegener's subject was never very large.

Wegener was a wonderful teacher. His students liked him for his frank, unpretentious manner and appreciated his clear explanations. Wegener was at the forefront of research in his field and he freely shared new findings with his students. In 1911 he published a meteorology textbook, *Thermodynamics of the Atmosphere*. The book was popular and went through several editions, which helped supplement Wegener's meager income.

During these years at Marburg, Wegener was also thinking about the fit of the continents. He wasn't the first to notice the matched contours of South America and Africa. Ever since the sixteenth century, when navigators circled and charted the globe, people had remarked on it. But Wegener connected this simple observation with a list of other troubling questions about why the world was the way it was: Why are the continents spaced so unevenly around the globe, with eighty percent of the land clustered in the Northern Hemisphere? Why do mountain chains often line the edges of continents? What causes mountains to form in the first place? Rock formations and fossils showed that the climate in many places on Earth had once been very different from today's climate. Fossils of tropical animals and plants turned up in present-day cold regions. What caused the climate change?

The common explanation was that Earth had formed from molten rock that had been cooling ever since. Therefore, the Earth of former eras had been much warmer overall, allowing warmth-loving species to flourish everywhere. As Earth aged, it cooled; as it cooled it contracted. Earth's contracting core caused the crust to wrinkle up just like the skin of a dried apple. The wrinkles on Earth's surface were mountain ranges. As Earth's core shrunk, the crust collapsed into the hollow in some places, causing oceans to form. That was the theory.

Many scientists accepted this idea of a cooling, contracting Earth. But when Wegener thought about it, it just didn't make sense to him. If mountains were formed by a shrivelling crust, why weren't mountains spaced out evenly all over the planet? Geologists also knew that mountain ranges had formed at different times. If the ranges formed as Earth cooled, they all should have risen up at the same time in the cooling process.

In 1911, Wegener happened to read a book about the striking similarity between fossils and living animals found in both Africa and South America. For example, mesosaurs, an extinct type of aquatic reptile, had lived on both continents. By Wegener's time, Darwin's theory of evolution was widely accepted. Here was a puzzle. What are the chances that the same animal evolved on two widely separated continents? It seemed impossible that random changes and natural selection would produce the very same result twice.

Many scientists believed that land bridges had once connected some of the continents. These land bridges would have allowed animals to cross from one continent to another. Then, at some time in the past, the bridges had sunk or collapsed into the ocean. Land

Fossils of mesosaurs from the Permian period have been found on the continents of South America and Africa. The discoveries led Wegener to believe that the two continents had once been part of one gigantic landmass.

bridges did not seem believable to Wegener, either. He couldn't picture a land bridge stretching all the way from South America to Africa—the distance was simply too great. He also didn't think animals such as snails, which were found on both sides, could have survived such a crossing.

Wegener began researching. A great deal of information had accumulated in the decades since Charles Lyell's time. In the nineteenth century, an educated man could master several sciences. In the twentieth century, the increasing mass of knowledge caused scientific fields such as geology to branch into many sub-specialities. Lyell could classify fossils, unravel the history of land formations and identify rocks and minerals. In present-day terms, he would be a paleontologist, a geomorphologist, and a mineralogist. Wegener was not expert in any branch of geology. He was a trained astronomer and a practicing meteorologist. But he was also determined to solve a problem and willing to venture into any field that could shed light on it

Because Marburg was a small university, Wegener shared ideas with professors in other departments, especially geology. These colleagues guided him through the research in their fields. Wegener wrote, "I require a lot of material for the work I'm doing. The geologists hunt up everything I need and give it to me, so that I am relieved of nine-tenths of the work. Otherwise I would need months to get as far as I have now."

Wegener read the work of Eduard Suess, an Austrian geologist who had studied the Alps. Suess divided the earth into three main layers, each composed of different materials: the outer crust of silicon-aluminum, called *sial*; the next layer of silicon-magnesium, called *sima*; and a core of nickel-iron, called *nife*. According to Suess, each layer is denser and heavier than the one above it. His idea that the continental crust is lighter than the layer underneath it, helped Wegener envision continents of sial floating on top of the heavier sima.

Another geological concept important to Wegener's theory is

isostasy. Isostasy is the property that land masses respond to pressure. If erosion or the retreat of a glacier removes mass from the top of a continent, for example, the continent will rebound; it will rise up. The bulge G. K Gilbert found in the center of Lake Bonneville is an example of isostatic rebound. If weight is added to a continent, by something like a glacier, it sinks down. Instead of being immobile and rigid, continental masses act something like Silly Putty over long, long periods of time. Wegener reasoned, if continents can move vertically, sinking and rising, why couldn't they also move horizontally?

WEGENER'S THEORY OF A SUPERCONTINENT

By 1912 Wegener had drawn information from many different fields into one comprehensive theory. He wrote a paper, "The Geophysical Basis of the Evolution of the Large-Scale Features of the Earth's Crust (Continents and Oceans)," which he presented to a meeting of the Geological Association in Frankfurt. He proposed that 250 million years ago, following the Carboniferous Period, all of the continents were joined together in one supercontinent. He called it Pangaea, which means "all-land."

According to Wegener, during the Triassic Period, Pangaea broke into huge pieces, which drifted across the globe to the positions the continents have today. The drifting continental masses were made of sial. Underneath this sial crust and under the waters of the oceans lay the heavier, denser sima. The sial moved, as if it were floating, across the sima.

Wegener's theory could explain the distribution of animals in both Africa and South America. The animals had once lived on Pangaea and continued to live on the separate pieces when the supercontinent broke up. It also explained the formation of mountain ranges. In the drift after the breakup, some land masses collided with each other. The Himalayan mountains were pushed up when present-day India jammed into Asia. The Andes rose on the leading edge of the westward-drifting South American continent. The theory accounted for climate changes. Many areas once had warmer climates because they had occupied a different part of the globe, closer to the equator, as part of Pangaea.

This first airing of Wegener's theory didn't produce much reaction from the scientific world, but he wasn't waiting for a reaction. That same year, he took a break from teaching to join a second expedition to Greenland. This expedition included only four men. Wegener and the leader, Johan Peter Koch, had worked together on the first Greenland trip—the Mylius-Erichsen expedition. One of the goals of the first trip had been to winter over on the ice sheet. Mylius-Erichsen had brought sled dogs to carry their equipment, but learned that the dogs could not climb the steep, icy slopes at its edge.

Koch was determined to set up his camp on the ice sheet for the second trip. Instead of dogs, he brought sixteen ponies from Iceland. These rugged little animals were able to make the climb, but all four men nearly died in the process. The glacier they were climbing suddenly began calving, that is a huge chunk split off and dropped into the sea. The four men narrowly escaped falling with it. The Koch expedition became the first to spend an entire winter on Greenland's ice sheet. They followed up with another first: a 1200 km (750 mile) trek across Greenland, from their winter campsite on the east side to Proven on the west side.

The journey over barren snow and icy peaks up to ten thousand feet (3000 m) was extremely dangerous. One by one the ponies died. The men had grown very fond of their animal companions. When the last pony was too weak to walk, Wegener tried pulling it on a sled, but he was not able to save it. The men themselves barely survived. Some Inuit found them, weak and nearly out of food, and helped them into Proven.

For Wegener, the 1912-13 expedition was a great scientific achievement. He had collected a wealth of new information about polar meteorology and succeeded in tracking storms across the ice cap for the first time. He had also taken spectacular photographs of beautiful arcs, auroras, and halos created by light in the icy atmosphere. He described standing there, " . . . under the flickering northern lights, with an overwhelming feeling of insignificance at the sight of this phenomenon of nature . . . . Above us the shining curtain unfolded in mysterious movements, a powerful symphony of light played in deepest, most solemn silence above our heads, as if mocking our efforts: Come up here and investigate me! Tell me what I am!"

Wegener's reputation in his field was secure; his career prospects were promising. In 1913 he married Else Koppen, daughter of the respected meteorologist Wladimir Koppen. Else was a bright woman, supportive of her husband's work. Alfred and Else Wegener worked together to publish an account of the 1912-13 Greenland expedition in German. Else also translated Koch's account of the trip from Danish into German; *Durch die Weisse Wuste* (*Across the White Wilderness*) was published in Berlin in 1919.

In the summer of 1914, Germany declared war on Russia and France and invaded Belgium. The complex of alliances between nations pulled country after country into The Great War. Wegener was conscripted to fight in the invading German army. His travels in Greenland had left him very fit. When Wegener was shot through the arm in Belgium, he recovered quickly and was sent back into combat. Two weeks later, a bullet lodged in his neck. In some ways it was a fortunate injury, for it gave him time to work, and kept him from further combat where he could have been killed later on. During his long recovery, Wegener filled the time with more work on Pangaea. In 1915 he published a fuller, more detailed account of his continental drift theory entitled *Die Entstehung der Kontinente und Ozeane* (*The Origin of Continents and Oceans*). Coming out in wartime Germany, the book did not reach a wide audience.

Because he was now unfit for combat, Wegener was re-assigned to the military weather service. When a meteorite came blazing down somewhere north of Germany, Wegener calculated its probable impact zone. The meteorite was found where Wegener predicted it would be. He became interested in the moon's craters and experimented with producing impact craters in powdered cement.

In 1919, after the war ended, the German Marine Observatory in Hamburg, Germany, invited Wegener to head their Department of Theoretical Meteorology. The previous department head, his father-in-law Wladimir Koppen, was retiring. Wegener's brother Kurt also headed a department there. Wegener accepted and moved his family to Hamburg. For the next five years, Wegener worked in the observatory, taught courses at the University of Hamburg, wrote *The Origin of the Moon Craters* (1921), and collaborated with his father-in-law on a new work, *Climates of the Geological Past* (1924). Wegener's father-in-law had also done pioneering work in studies of the atmosphere. He was both immensely learned and intellectually daring. In fact, Wegener had first met his future wife Else while visiting her father to talk over his work in Greenland.

At first, Koppen did not accept Wegener's ideas about continental drift. But he could not dismiss the theory, either. Else Wegener wrote, "My father always carried a small globe in his coat pocket, in order to be able to think about this idea at any time." Eventually, Koppen came to be one of Wegener's firmest supporters. Wegener's theory explained so many puzzling facts. Their book, *Climates of the Geological Past*, applies the theory of continental drift to the very confusing problem of climate history.

The evidence for past climates consists of plant and animal fossils and rocks, such as desert sandstone, which form only under specific climatic conditions. Up until this time, climatologists noted the distribution of this evidence, but couldn't come up with a consistent explanation for it. For example, *Glossopteris*, a primitive fern found in cool climates, had once grown in India, Australia, and South Africa—places that are now warm. There were also signs that glaciers had once covered parts of all these landmasses. Similarly, coal deposits, the remains of swampy Carboniferous forests that grew in warm, tropical and subtropical climates, occurred in seemingly unrelated locations in Europe and North America.

Wegener and Koppen plotted all these rock and fossil features on a reconstructed map of Pangaea. Distribution patterns that had looked random before, now lined up in clear climatic zones. Glacial deposits in southern Africa, Australia, South America, and India were united on the Pangaean supercontinent near the South Pole. Carboniferous forests flourished around the equator. Formations of salt and desert sandstone clustered in dry regions. Even opponents of the theory had to admire the solutions it offered to climate mysteries.

Wegener never stopped working on continental drift. He published two more editions of *The Origin of Continents and Oceans* (*OCO*), adding more supporting evidence. The third edition, published in 1922, was translated into English, French, Russian, Spanish, and Swedish. Finally, Wegener's idea was reaching an international audience.

The more scientists it reached, however, the more opponents lined up against Wegener. For many scientists, the idea that continents could move was startling. As one scientist remarked, "If we are to believe [this] hypothesis, we must forget everything we have learned in the last 70 years and start all over again." This is exactly what Wegener expected to happen. He wrote to his father-in-law, "If it turns out that sense and meaning are now becoming evident in the whole history of the earth's development, why should we hesitate to toss the old views overboard?"

Wegener's vast vision of Earth's past also rankled scientists entrenched in their specialties. Wegener was an outsider; he had no credentials in geology or geophysics or paleontology. Specialists didn't trust his work. Where did he get the authority to turn all these fields upside-down? Wegener's theory was attacked and ridiculed. One writer termed it "a fairy tale." Another called it, " . . . the fantasy of a geophysicist . . . that would pop like a soap bubble." But Wegener's idea was too sturdy to pop like a soap bubble; and Wegener himself was calmly confident—even obstinate—about continental drift.

Many of those who didn't accept Wegener's theory still found it brilliant. Those who dismissed it still felt they had to respond to it. A gathering of scientists debated the theory at a symposium in England in 1922 and at a second symposium in New York in 1926. Proponents of the new theory were called *mobilists*. Opponents, who believed the continents were fixed firmly in place, were called *fixists*.

The big question about continental drift, the end focus of these debates, was always, how: What force could move continents? Wegener had various suggestions. One was "pohl-flucht," the pole-fleeing force, the idea that mass on a rotating sphere like Earth, is gradually forced away from the poles and toward the equator. He also suggested that tides and Earth's rotation could combine to cause the westward drift of the Americas. But Wegener himself had to say that neither of these suggestions was convincing. He wrote, "It is probable that complete solution of the problem of the driving forces will still be a long time coming."

The weight of opinion on both sides of the Atlantic went against Wegener, although he had some steadfast supporters. A few scientists favored the theory because it explained the things they saw. Some Swiss geologists found it useful in explaining the Alps. Continental drift also made sense to Dutch geologists who were familiar with their country's Indonesian territories. South African geologist Alexander du Toit had been struck by the numerous similarities in geology between his country and South America.

Arthur Holmes, a British geologist, also liked the idea of continental drift. Holmes had pioneered the use of radioactive decay methods to find the age of rocks, an important tool in geology. Now he had the idea of a driving force to explain continental drift. Holmes suggested that slow convection currents of molten material in Earth's mantle, the layer under the crust, could move the continents above and thus power continental drift. Since most of the scientific world rejected Wegener's theory, they had no need of Holmes's idea, either. More than thirty years would go by before these theories began to be accepted.

The reaction against Wegener's theory was particularly strong in

Germany. After several German universities turned him down, Wegener realized he would never be offered a teaching position there. In 1924, the University of Graz in Austria invited him to become a professor of meteorology and geophysics. Wegener accepted. The Wegener household now included his wife, three young daughters, and his father- and mother-in-law. They moved to Graz, where Wegener became an Austrian citizen.

In 1929, he published a fourth edition of *OCO*. Since its original publication in 1915, the book had expanded from 94 to 231 pages. He had compiled more evidence, citing more similarities between continents, such as the gneiss plateaus found in Brazil and across the ocean in Africa; and the Old Red Sandstone, a rock formation extending from the Baltics through Great Britain, Greenland, and the United States. He also included the fact that manatees live in the waters off both Central America and west Africa, but can't survive in the deep ocean in between.

Wegener used geodetic measurements—measurements pinpointing exact locations on the globe. Measurements taken in 1823 and in 1907 seemed to show that Greenland was drifting away from Europe at a rate of approximately thirty-two meters (105 feet) a year. Unfortunately, instruments measuring longitude were not very accurate. None of the geodetic data available to Wegener were reliable; however, the idea was sound. Today satellite measurements show that Greenland is indeed moving west, but at only two cm (less than an inch) per year.

Wegener also kept up with new work in meteorology. His former student and friend Johannes Georgi was planning to go to Greenland to study the jet stream. When the expedition's funding organization asked Wegener to lead the expedition, he was happy to accept.

Wegener planned to set up three camps: a base camp on the west coast; a second camp in the middle of the ice sheet; and a third camp on the east coast. Over a two-year stay, the expedition could thoroughly study the weather and atmosphere across the entire land

Before Wegener began an expedition, he made careful plans and compiled information that he wanted to test through observations in the field.

mass. Through 1928 and 1929, Wegener rushed to arrange funding, choose his scientific team, and order instruments and supplies. From past experience, Wegener knew that careful planning could become a matter of life and death during the Greenland winter. Previous expedition leaders had tried dogs and ponies to help transport supplies onto the ice sheet. Wegener decided to add something new; he purchased two special motorized sleds in Finland.

In 1929 Wegener made a preliminary trip to Greenland with three of his expedition members. They studied the western coastline

This was the last photo of Wegener taken before he left on his 1930 expedition to Greenland.

and chose the spot for their base camp. They also tried out a new technique for measuring the thickness of the ice sheet. First, they set off explosives. Some distance away, a research team waited with a seismometer, an instrument that detects vibrations moving through Earth. They tracked how long it took for the force of the explosion to register on the seismograph. This measurement told them how long it had taken the waves released by the explosion to travel down through the ice, bounce off the underlying rock and travel back up to their location. Wegener and his team were the first to use this technique in polar research.

THE END OF ALFRED WEGENER'S LIFE

Wegener returned from this scouting expedition in the fall of 1929. There were only a few frantic months to complete his final preparations for the full expedition. On April 1, 1930, Wegener and twenty expedition members set out from Copenhagen, Denmark, for the west coast of Greenland. On arrival, the expedition faced a disaster. Sheets of sea ice locked every approach to their landing point. Their ship was not able to plow through to the coast for six full weeks. Wegener knew the expedition was losing precious time, the time they needed to supply their camps before winter set in. On June 9, he wrote in his journal, "Our expedition's program is slowly being seriously jeopardized by the obstinacy of the ice."

On June 16 they were finally able to land and begin unloading their ninety-eight tons of supplies; building a road to the glacier's sides; hiring sled drivers and dog teams; and paying Greenlanders to supply dried shark meat for the dogs and hay for the ponies. Then came another delay. The motorized sleds didn't have enough power to climb the ice slopes. All the supplies for the Mid-Ice station would have to be hauled, more slowly and with more effort, by ponies instead.

Wegener seemed tireless to his men, but in his journal he wrote, "Life here has its dark side. A person wouldn't be able to put up with most of it, if he didn't know that after a certain number of months are marked off on the calendar, he can go back home . . . And then, thank goodness, the obligation to be a hero ends, too. . . . Even a paradise eventually loses its ability to make a person happy. I can see the time coming when it will be like that for me with Greenland."

On July 16, meteorologist Johannes Georgi and glaciologist Ernest Sorge went inland 400 km (250 miles) to set up the Mid-Ice camp. They waited there for supplies: a hut for the winter; fuel; a radio transmitter; a winter's store of food. But by the time Wegener and his men got the supplies up onto the ice sheet and set up West Station, bad weather was setting in. The sleds wouldn't work. Too much time had been lost.

Wegener was worried about the two men at Mid-Ice. He didn't think they had gotten in enough supplies to last the long winter. Moreover, he knew that without a dog sled, they would die trying to come back to base camp. On September 21, he set out with fifteen dogsleds loaded with supplies. A terrible storm with driving snow and high winds made it nearly impossible to keep going. At night the temperatures dropped to -50°C (-58°F). All but one of the Inuit driving the dogsleds turned back.

The trip, which usually took twenty days, took forty punishing days. Wegener reached Mid-Ice on October 30, with two companions and three empty dogsleds—no food, no radio, no fuel, no equipment. One of his men had such severe frostbite on his feet that he would not be able to make the trip back to West Station. He would have to spend the winter at Mid-Ice, stretching their supplies to feed one more man.

Wegener found that Georgi and Sorge had dug down into the ice and hollowed out a cave-shelter. The ceiling was low, the space cramped and dark, but after forty days in a storm, Wegener was delighted with it. They had also carefully rationed their food supply to make it last through the winter. Much of the equipment they had planned on using had never reached Mid-Ice, but they were making all the observations that they could. Their resourcefulness cheered Wegener.

Wegener knew that the scanty food at Mid-Ice would barely sustain three men for the winter, let alone five. He and Rasmus Villumsen, a rugged and loyal Greenlander, had to return to West Station. On November 1, 1930, Wegener's fiftieth birthday, they set out with seventeen dogs. The men at Mid-Ice would not have any further contact with the outside world until the end of winter came in May or June. On December 13, Else Wegener received a letter from her husband. He had written it on September 20, the day before he started for Mid-Ice. After that, there were no more letters.

Wegener never made it back to West Station. It was too dangerous to send out a rescue party. The men there simply hoped he had

*In order to measure the temperature of the ice, Wegener bored a hole
in the ice sheet and took out samples.*

decided not to risk the return trip and stayed at Mid-Ice. In May 1931, the expedition members found a pair of skis sticking up out of the snow about halfway between the two stations. The skis marked Wegener's grave. He had probably died of a heart attack from extreme exertion. Villumsen had carefully stitched the body into two sleeping bag covers and dug a grave in the ice. He had taken Wegener's notebook, probably intending to bring it to West Station, but Villumsen never made it back, either. His body was never found. The men set up an iron cross, six meters high, over Wegener's grave, but today, even this marker is buried under the ice.

The members of the expedition stayed in Greenland to complete their research. Wegener's brother Kurt took over as expedition leader to finish Alfred's work. Alfred Wegener was honored in Germany and Austria as a great explorer. A German institute for polar research; a peninsula in western Greenland; a road in Hamburg and one in Graz are all named for him. But Wegener's work on continental drift lay largely ignored and discredited for the next thirty years.

In the 1950s, new techniques made it possible to map the ocean floor and uncover the history of changes in Earth's magnetic field. The new data revealed that Wegener had been right about the continents: they move. They don't move in exactly the way he envisioned; "continental drift" is not exactly the right term. But his overall theory had been brilliantly ahead of its time.

Wegener believed that the ocean floor was denser than the continents and that it was immobile, that the lighter continents moved across it. He was half right. The ocean floor is generally denser than the continental crust; however, the ocean floor is not immobile. The whole surface of the earth, continents and ocean floor, is a mosaic of huge irregularly-shaped pieces called *tectonic plates*. It is these plates, made up of both land and ocean floor, that move. They drift and jostle against each other all around the globe.

What propels them? Scientist still don't agree on the answer to this question. Holmes's idea of convection currents in the underlying mantle seems most likely. As Wegener protested in the 1920s, many phenomena are accepted long before they are completely understood.

A major advance in understanding the ways in which pieces of Earth's surface move around came from American geologist Harry Hess. After studying the ocean floor himself and examining data collected by many scientists, Hess put forward a theory called seafloor spreading. Hess suggested that new molten material constantly wells up at the ridge. This molten rock cools and hardens, forming new ocean crust at the ridge, and then moves away to either side, like a huge, slow conveyor belt. When Hess first wrote up his idea, he himself called it "geopoetry."

Hess's discovery has helped reveal an Earth less "fixed" and more mobile than even Wegener envisioned. Once people were convinced that seafloor spreading occurred, then they could believe that the continents moved as well. Although he didn't succeed in his lifetime, Wegener forced people to think about radically new possibilities. He confronted a scientific mystery with tremendous force of imagination, breadth of research, and confidence in the truth of his work. Wegener didn't outlast his critics; but his work did. Honored in his own time as an explorer and meteorologist, Wegener now has a firm place in the history of geology as the "father of continental drift."

5 "Splitting Apart at the Seam"

HARRY HESS AND THE THEORY OF SEAFLOOR SPREADING

It was 1931. Twenty-five-year-old Harry Hess was a researcher on the USS *Barracuda,* a submarine in the U.S. Navy. Hess and the crew were more than ready for their shore leave in Santiago, Cuba. It had been a rough trip, one Hess was not likely to forget.

The *Barracuda* was the oldest submarine in the Navy. Some people even said that it had already sunk once and had just been salvaged. On one dive, something malfunctioned and the sub began to descend at a very steep angle. Submarines cannot dive to infinite depths because the water pressure becomes so great that it can crush the ship. Fortunately, the problem was fixed before the submarine had descended too deeply and it was able to rise to the surface. On another occasion, while in the Caribbean sea, the skipper put up the periscope just to make sure no other ships were nearby (it was very unlikely), and found himself looking straight at the hull of a huge ocean liner. They quickly dove and missed getting ripped apart by just a few feet.

Life in a cramped submarine is not particularly pleasant, so Hess and a friend were thrilled when they arrived at Santiago and checked into the best room in town. They had a spectacular,

Harry Hess (1906–1969)

panoramic view of the city. But land was no more stable than the sea—about 2:00 A.M. an earthquake shook the island and demolished the front of the hotel.

What was Harry Hess, a graduate student in geology, doing on a submarine in the first place? He was collecting information about the Caribbean seafloor. And although he didn't know it at the time, Hess was beginning his work on the most revolutionary theory in Earth sciences: plate tectonics.

THE YOUNG HARRY HESS

Harry Hammond Hess was born in New York City on May 24, 1906. He and his brother, Frank, grew up in New York City where his father worked on the Stock Exchange, and his grandfather was in the dredging business.

In 1923, Hess entered Yale University. He started off studying electrical engineering, but after a couple of years he got tired of "drawing cross sections of spark plugs." He decided to try geology instead. Hess didn't do very well at first; one of his professors actually told him that he had no future in geology. Fortunately, Hess didn't give up.

After he graduated in 1928, Hess went to Southern Rhodesia (now known as Zimbabwe) to work for a mining company. The company made the geologists walk seventeen miles a day, back and forth in a sort of grid pattern, making geological maps of the area and looking for signs of mineral deposits. To Hess it was silly work. He could have accomplished the same thing much more efficiently if the company had trusted him to decide where to look.

Hess decided to return to the United States and attend graduate school. He really wanted to go to Harvard, but when he went to visit the campus, he was met with an unbearable sight: no smoking signs were posted on every wall. Hess was a chain smoker and couldn't imagine not being able to indulge whenever and wherever he wanted. So, he decided to try for Princeton instead. According to Hess, it was a lucky break that he was accepted at Princeton. One of the professors there remembered him lecturing on Cambrian geology to his drinking companions on a field trip.

At Princeton, Hess worked with some extraordinary professors in several very different fields. He studied mineralogy, petrology (rocks), mineral deposits, and the structure of the ocean basin. Later on, Hess would combine information from these seemingly unrelated fields in one revolutionary theory.

In 1931, Hess's oceanography professor arranged for him to go out on the *Barracuda*. Hess joined the Dutch geophysicist Felix A. Vening-Meinesz on this submarine mission to study gravity over the Caribbean.

Geologists know that the force of gravity is not uniform; in some places on Earth, the pull of gravity is greater than in others. The pull of gravity between two objects depends on their masses. Gravity is greater for more massive objects; this is why people weigh more on Earth than they do on the moon—Earth is more massive than the moon. Gravity is slightly greater over mountains than over valleys because rock is denser (and therefore more massive) than air. Dense rock exerts a stronger gravitational pull than less dense rock. So measuring variations in the gravitational pull is a way of learning about the rock deep in Earth's crust.

In the 1920s, Vening-Meinesz developed a way to measure gravity at sea using two or three pendulums. The time it takes for the pendulums to swing back and forth varies with variations in gravity. Vening-Meinesz had to use the instrument on a submarine because surface ships rolled around too much. Hess had the frustrating task of trying to start both pendulums swinging at exactly the same time in order to start the gravity-meter. As the submarine cruised from the deep Atlantic, westwards into the Caribbean Sea, Vening-Meinesz and Hess measured gravity all along the way.

They were especially interested in the gravity over deep sea trenches. These trenches are long, narrow, and very deep valleys along the edges of the ocean floor. (The lowest place on Earth, 11,033 meters (36,198 feet) below sea-level, is in the Marianas Trench in the Pacific Ocean; a stack of twenty-five Empire State Buildings could be placed in this trench.) These trenches aren't straight; they are curved. Geologists noticed two strange things about these trenches. First, there are chains of volcanoes along the inside edges of curving ocean trenches. In the Caribbean, an arc of islands called the Lesser Antilles strings along the western edge of a sea trench. Secondly, a large number of very powerful earthquakes (including the one the crew was to experience in Cuba) occur near trenches.

Measurements showed that the pull of gravity over the Caribbean trench was surprisingly weak. Because they thought that trenches cut deep into the underlying rock, the geologists expected gravity to be less there than over normal depths, but they didn't expect it to be *this* low. What did that tell Vening-Meinesz and Hess? It told them that the trench was not a simple valley—there was something strange going on deeper in the crust. Perhaps, in fact, the ocean crust was warping downwards.

When Hess got back on land he finished his Ph.D. The subject was not his gravity work on the ocean crust with Vening-Meinesz. Instead, he had studied some rocks called peridotites in the Blue Ridge Mountains of Virginia. Little did Hess know that this was much more related to ocean trenches than he thought. Some mountain peridotite bodies are now thought to be pieces of oceanic crust, plastered to the continents during continental collisions.

Like most people who get Ph.D.s in geology today, Hess spent several years at various institutions before landing a permanent teaching position. After he graduated from Princeton, Hess taught for a year at Rutgers University in New Jersey. Then he went to the Geophysical Laboratory of the Carnegie Institution of Washington, D.C., to continue doing research. In 1934 he returned to Princeton as a teacher.

Less than ten years later an event occurred that took Hess out of the classroom. On December 7, 1941, the Japanese attacked Pearl Harbor, on the island of Oahu, Hawaii. This event brought the United States into World War II. The United States declared war on Japan and Germany. The next morning Hess, who was a reserve officer in the Navy, took the train from Princeton to New York City to report for active duty. Because German subs had been sinking U.S. convoys in the northern Atlantic, the commander of the Eastern Sea Frontier needed men with submarine experience. Hess began his wartime work as an antisubmarine warfare officer.

One problem was that the U.S. Navy was not able to spot German subs as they surfaced to make radio communications. Hess knew about a warm current of water that ran from the Gulf of Mexico, up along the U.S. coast, and across the Atlantic south of Greenland—the Gulf Stream. The Navy knew about the Gulf Stream as well, but did not understand its significance. Hess knew that there was a low bank of clouds that formed in the Atlantic just north of

During World War II, U.S. Navy Commander Hess figured out ways to spot enemy submarines. He also made important discoveries while mapping the ocean floor.

the Gulf Stream. He figured that the German subs surfaced below those clouds, where planes (which did not yet have radar) couldn't spot them. The U.S. Navy took Hess's suggestion and sent bombers out to that part of the Atlantic to drop depth charges. Within twelve months, there were almost no German subs left in the Atlantic.

Hess had been able to use his knowledge of geology to help the war effort. He also took advantage of his position in the Navy to learn more about the geology of the ocean floor. Hess really wanted to go back out to sea, but his requests were continually denied. The Navy needed his expertise on land. Eventually though he did get to go to sea.

In 1943 Hess was ordered to report to Los Angeles to help re-model the transport ship USS *Cape Johnson*. He was able to spend his time installing a deep-sea echo sounder. An echo sounder sends a "ping" down from the ship to the seafloor and listens for the echo. By measuring the time it takes for the "ping" to echo back, one can calculate the depth of the seafloor. The greater the distance from the ship to the seafloor, the longer it takes for the echo to bounce back. By plotting thousands of measurements, a bathymetric map, a map showing the contours of the seafloor, can be made. Most ships had instruments to measure shallow depths, in places like bays and harbors, but few had instruments for the deep sea. Hess insisted on having one on his ship.

Eventually the USS *Cape Johnson* was ready for sea. Officially, the ship was used to transport troops to various battlegrounds in the Pacific, which were on islands such as the Marianas, Leyte, and Iwo Jima. Unofficially, it was Commander Harry Hess's own personal survey ship. He used the echo sounder whenever he could. This doesn't seem like such a courageous feat, but it was dangerous—the "ping" sound sent down to the seafloor could alert Japanese submarines to the ship's presence. Looking at the *Cape Johnson's* routes, a ship captain would have assumed that the ship was continually weaving around to outwit submarines. But an experienced geologist would notice that the back and forth, zigzagging, overlapping routes matched interesting parts of the seafloor.

Commander Hess gathered data until the very end of the war, when about twenty ships were headed from the Philippines to Japan. To communicate with one another, the ships used semaphore flags. The signalmen needed practice, so Hess suggested that all the ships continuously record the ocean depth and then report their observations every hour. The fleet of ships came home safely, with a swath of bathymetry (depth measurements) ten miles wide (16 km) and two thousand miles (3,200 km) long.

HESS DISCOVERS GUYOTS

Hess made an interesting discovery while mapping the Pacific ocean floor. He found that it was dotted with flat-topped mountains called seamounts, like rocky cones with their tops cut off. Some of them were under more than ten thousand feet (3,000 meters) of water. Hess mapped more than 160 seamounts and named them "guyots," after Arnold Guyot, who founded Princeton's geology department in 1854. Hess didn't know exactly what guyots were, but he suspected that they were ancient volcanoes, probably more than 600 million years old. He figured they had erupted, forming islands of lava that rose out of the ocean, then waves had worn away the volcano tops. Finally, as the continents eroded, dumping sediments into the sea, the sea level had risen and drowned the islands. It was a reasonable interpretation, but not completely right. A few years later he would learn the fascinating truth about guyots.

In the days of Charles Lyell or G. K. Gilbert, a geologist, working alone, could walk the terrain and make significant discoveries. Lyell could climb Mount Etna to study its layers; Gilbert could map the contours of the ancient Lake Bonneville in Utah. But no geologist could walk the walls of a deep ocean trench. Direct observation was impossible.

Charles Lyell could look at an ancient fossil bed and imagine the swamp that must have been there. Geologists like Hess had to be able to translate columns of observations and measurements gathered by new and sophisticated instruments into a picture of the ocean floor. With the rapid developments in technology, geology had also become a very expensive science. New discoveries required teams of scientists and state-of-the-art equipment, funded by large institutions—museums, universities, and governments. This is one reason the story of Hess's work involves the work of so many other geologists, each supplying discoveries that helped Hess put together a new theory of the ocean floor.

In July 1950, a number of scientists (not including Hess) went on the Mid-Pacific Expedition to study the Pacific seafloor. Before the 1950s, geologists had ideas of what the seafloor and the ocean crust were like. Most geologists thought that the oceanic crust must be composed of thick sediments that accumulated over billions of years as the continents wore down. They believed that the oceanic crust would be the oldest crust on Earth, older than the continents. Moreover, they thought that except for a few mountains here and there, the ocean floor was very, very flat—it must be if it was all filled in with sediment. What they found was that many of their ideas were completely wrong.

The Mid-Pac science crew used explosives and seismic waves to measure the thickness of the sediment on the seafloor. It wasn't tens of thousands of meters thick as they expected. It was only several hundred meters thick. How could this be if the ocean floor was ancient?

When they tried to figure out how old the sediments were by looking at the fossils in them, they found that they were all relatively young. No sediments formed earlier than the Cretaceous period. They sailed over the seafloor and used an echo sounder to map the ocean floor. It wasn't smooth at all, but covered in small hills! When they used seismic waves to measure the thickness of the oceanic crust, it was not very thick: only seven km on average (four miles). By comparison, the continental crust is on average thirty-five km (twenty-two miles) thick.

The geologists on the cruise were also fascinated by Hess's discovery of guyots and decided to see if guyots really were drowned pre-Cambrian islands. They used echo sounders to find the guyots, and then used corers and dredges (metal bags on the end of cables, dragged behind the ship) to scoop up rocks and sediment. If Hess was right, these seamounts should be covered in a thick blanket of sand, mud, and gravel. And the hard rocks that made up the cores of the guyots should be more than 550 million years old. What they found instead was coral. Coral only grows in warm shallow water. What was it doing this deep? The coral was actually very old, but not nearly as old as Hess had imagined. It was all Cretaceous-aged, just 130 million years old or so, and younger.

This expedition was just one of many research cruises. Serious exploration of the oceans went on for the next decade. Two major features on the ocean floor were especially interesting: the high mid-ocean ridges, and the deep ocean trenches.

Scientists and explorers had known for some time that a broad spine, an underwater mountain range, ran down the middle of the Atlantic Ocean. In the 1850s, this "Middle Ground" was mapped by Matthew Maury, a lieutenant in the U.S. Navy. Several decades later, ships laying the trans-Atlantic cable noticed it as well. In 1954 Bruce Heezen of the Lamont Geological Observatory of Columbia University in New York (and later Maurice Ewing and Marie Tharp), discovered that the Mid-Atlantic Ridge was just one section of a global system. These ridges form a huge mountain chain that winds around Earth. It is more than sixty thousand kilometers (38,000 miles) long and rises as much as 4,500 meters (15,000 feet) off the seafloor. If there were no oceans obscuring them, the mid-ocean ridges would be the most prominent landform on Earth.

In the 1920s members of the German Meteor expedition to study the seafloor noticed a rift, or valley, in the middle of the Mid-Atlantic Ridge. Their discovery was virtually ignored until 1957, when Maurice Ewing (also from Lamont) noticed that the ridges have rifts running down the center. This was a very important discovery. It showed that ridges weren't like mountain chains on land, which are forced up by compression—when rock layers are pushed together. Instead, the rift marked a place where the ocean floor seems to have been pulled apart. Researchers also made another very important observation: there was fresh lava along the mid-ocean ridges, and virtually no sediment.

Ocean trenches were also interesting. Geologists wondered: Were they just submarine canyons? Were they cracks in the crust, formed by expansion of Earth? Or were they wrinkles, formed by compression? Earthquakes provided the answer. Seismologists noticed that earthquakes were not evenly scattered across Earth; instead, they were concentrated in belts. Many of the smaller earthquakes occurred along the mid-ocean ridges. But the deepest and the most powerful earthquakes occurred near the ocean trenches, in places such as Chile, Japan, and (as Hess had experienced) the Caribbean.

In the 1920s, the Japanese geophysicist Kiyoo Wadati showed that earthquakes near the Japan trench occur on a zone where the ocean floor dips down into Earth, away from the trench and towards Asia. Similar zones occur near other trenches. Twenty years later, Hugo Benioff determined that these earthquakes occur along a single fault zone where rocks have broken and are moving against each other. Near Peru and Chile it was a fault zone 4,500 km (2,800 miles) long and nine hundred km (560 miles) wide. In the Pacific, almost all of these fault zones dip away from the Pacific Ocean. These zones of earthquakes are now known as Wadati-Benioff zones.

Wadati and Benioff's discovery proved to be extremely important. It showed that the ocean trenches were located along faults that, for the most part, formed by compression. In these places, huge sections of crust were pushing up against each other. The faults seemed to be a result of large sections of crust being forced over and under one another.

Harry Hess, who was now a full professor at Princeton, kept a close watch on all the new information coming in from the oceans. Hess was a very busy man devoted to his work, but was also a dedicated husband and father to two sons. His friend William Rubey described him as a man of "cheery, unruffled temperament" with "puckish wit," a man who made committee meetings tolerable. John Maxwell, a graduate student and then colleague at Princeton, says he was soft-spoken and quiet, "just a prince." But others (especially scientists from other institutions) found him to be arrogant, cold, and distant. They complained that although he was generous with compliments when he spoke, he did not cite other scientists adequately in his papers. Like many scientists, Hess was enthusiastic, but aggressive about pursuing information and not always fair.

Alfred Wegener's theory of continental drift had been at the back of geologists' minds, but most still thought it was a farfetched idea. Hess kept his mind open. Along with oceanographic data, he was also aware of strange and interesting reports that were coming in from another field of geophysics: paleomagnetism.

Earth is like one big magnet. It has a north pole and a south pole. A compass works because a small needle made of a magnetic material, such as iron-oxide, aligns with Earth's magnetic field so that the needle points north. Small magnetic minerals in rocks do the same thing. When an igneous rock begins to cool and solidify, the magnetic minerals crystallizing in the rock become magnetized in the direction of Earth's magnetic field. When the rock cools, the orientation is locked in. Geologists recognized that they could use iron-rich rocks as fossil compasses. The rocks could tell them where the magnetic poles were in the past.

In the 1950s, some British geophysicists measured the direction in which some European rocks of different ages were magnetized. They noticed that there was a steady change in the direction. This suggested that perhaps Earth's poles had wandered over time. Then the geophysicists did the same measurements on North American rocks of the same age. The rocks showed the same wandering pattern.

Strangely enough, the exact locations of the pole were different between North American and European rocks. It looked as though the rocks in North America were aligned to one north pole, while the rocks in Europe were aligned to another. This seemed impossible. For younger rocks, the patterns and locations matched up exactly, as if there were then just one north pole. They quickly recognized that these patterns made sense if North America and Europe were together as one continent, and then started to split apart during the Mesozoic Era about 180 million years ago.

Rocks from Africa, South America, and Australia showed the same magnetic patterns. The polar wandering paths didn't make sense separately, but when the continents were put together as the great supercontinent Gondwanaland, they made perfect sense. Gondwanaland was Eduard Suess's name for the southern portion of Wegener's supercontinent, Pangaea. Although this evidence convinced only a few Earth scientists that continental drift was the answer, it did make them more tolerant to the idea.

HESS PROPOSES THE THEORY
OF SEAFLOOR SPREADING

Harry Hess thought about the mid-ocean ridge, how it seemed to be splitting apart, and how basaltic lava was erupting from it. He thought about the thin oceanic crust made of basalt. He thought about how there were thick sediments far away from the ridge, but none on it. He thought about guyots, which were deeper underwater the farther away they were from the mid-ocean ridge. He thought about the ocean trenches and the faults that showed that parts of the ocean crust were converging, causing one section to dive beneath another. It was all beginning to make sense. In 1959, Hess wrote a paper called "The History of Ocean Basins," in which he proposed an idea that is now known as "seafloor spreading."

Hess wrote that the oceanic crust was splitting apart at a seam: the mid-ocean ridge. He wrote that new oceanic crust forms at the ridge, and is then rafted away from either side. After millions of years it arrives at the trenches, and dives deep down into Earth. How did this work? Like Arthur Holmes thirty years before, Hess thought that the crust could be moved by convection currents in the mantle below.

The mantle is the dense, hot, solid layer of rock beneath Earth's crust. The deeper the rock, the hotter it is. Like all geologists, Hess knew that 1) even solid rock, if it is hot enough and given enough time, can flow like a fluid, and 2) hot rock is more buoyant than cold rock (because it is not as dense), so hot rock should rise and cool rock should sink.

Hess reasoned that the rock in Earth's mantle circulates slowly: hot material rises, cools off, sinks, heats up again, and rises again. This type of circulation is called convection. In his paper, Hess wrote that hot material in the mantle rises beneath the mid-ocean ridges. As it cools off, it moves horizontally in opposite directions, splitting the crust above and taking it along. Eventually the mantle rock cools off so much that it sinks, pulling the crust down with it, and forming an ocean trench. Unlike Wegener, who thought that the continents plowed through the mantle, Hess saw them ride passively over the convecting mantle, just as icebergs ride on an ocean current.

Even though the rocks of the mid-ocean ridge are continuously being broken and rafted away, the ridge itself stays. It is continuously replenished by the mantle below. As the mantle rock rises below the ridge, part of it melts. New ocean crust forms when some of this magma erupts as lava on the ocean floor, and some solidifies below. The process continues as the mantle currents carry this newly formed rock away from the ridge. Guyots form close to the ridge and are then rafted away towards the trenches with the rest of the ocean crust.

Hess knew that much of what he wrote was just theory. The evidence collected so far supported the idea, but still he wrote, "I shall consider this paper an essay in geopoetry." Hess's idea was fairly well received when it was published in 1962. It made sense to those who were studying the ocean floor. In fact, Robert S. Dietz, a geologist with the Scripps Institution of Oceanography in San Diego, had published almost the exact same theory the year before. (Did one man steal the other's idea? Or did they both come up with the same idea independently? Different people have said different things.) But it wasn't until the next year that the real clincher came.

There was yet another strange aspect to magnetized rocks: some of them were magnetized in the direction exactly opposite to what one would expect, as if the north and south poles were reversed. Geophysicists noticed that there was a correlation between the ages of the rocks and which direction they were magnetized. It wasn't just that some rocks were oriented one way, and others the other way, but that rocks of a certain age were all magnetized in the same direction. This implied that every so often the magnetic poles switched: the south pole became the north pole and the north pole became the south pole. In 1963 geologists found that the results were consistent around the world. Rocks less than 750,000 years old are magnetized normally, but those between 750,000 and about 925,000 years old are reversely magnetized. So it wasn't a fluke. It looked as though the poles do flip every few million years.

Among all of their other studies, oceanographers measured the magnetics of the seafloor. Since it is mostly made of basalt, and basalt is composed of iron-rich minerals that are easily magnetized, the ocean floor was an ideal place to study. This was done (and still is) by towing a magnetometer about one hundred meters (325 feet) behind the ship. With a magnetometer, they can determine whether the rocks are magnetized normally or reversed.

What the oceanographers found was very interesting. The ocean floors weren't all magnetized the same way, but they also weren't magnetized in a random or chaotic fashion. There were magnetic stripes on the seafloor. As they sailed across the ocean, perpendicular to a mid-ocean ridge, ships would cross a section of normal magnetization several hundred km across, then they would cross a reversely magnetized area. Then the rocks would be normal again. When all the magnetic information from all the ships was mapped, a zebra pattern of magnetic "stripes" was apparent.

In 1962 Harry Hess visited Cambridge University in England, to give a talk on seafloor spreading and the evolution of the North Atlantic Ocean. Fred Vine, a college student at Cambridge, loved the talk and couldn't get the idea of seafloor spreading out of his head. Vine was trying to explain the strange magnetic striping on either side of the Carlsberg Ridge in the Indian Ocean. Only one scenario suited him—Hess's seafloor spreading. Vine reasoned that when magma cooled and created new ocean crust at the mid-ocean ridges, it was magnetized in the direction of the current magnetic field. The crust was then carried away from either side of the ridge. When the magnetic poles switched, the new crust took on a reverse magnetization. The seafloor was like one big magnetic tape recorder! Vine wrote up a draft of his ideas.

Today, this interpretation is obvious. But then it was a crazy idea and scientists didn't immediately take to it. (One certainly liked it: a Canadian geologist, Lawrence Morley, who had read Dietz's paper on seafloor spreading and came up with the same hypothesis as Vine). Vine was thrilled when Harry Hess came to Cambridge in 1965 and told him that he thought the hypothesis was a fantastic idea. No one had ever said that to him before. In 1966, when scientists confirmed that the patterns were exactly parallel to the mid-ocean ridges and that they were exactly symmetrical in both magnetics and age, most geologists finally accepted that large-scale lateral movement of Earth's crust is very real and very important.

HARRY HESS'S ACHIEVEMENTS

When Alfred Wegener proposed that the continents drift across Earth's surface, his idea was rejected by almost everyone. No one wanted to accept the idea of moving land masses. Forty years later, technology made it possible to study the secrets of the ocean floor. Many scientists made important discoveries that overturned every previous assumption about the oceanic crust.

Harry Hess had the imagination and grasp of data to put these discoveries together in a new comprehensive theory. His theory of seafloor spreading also explained what Wegener couldn't—what force could move a continent. As Hess saw it, continents don't plow across a stable sea floor. Instead, continents and seafloor together are carried along by the slow, yet powerful churning of the mantle. Far from being the oldest, most unchanging feature of Earth, the seafloor is an area of constant change, ever renewed at the up-welling ridge, and ever destroyed in the downwelling near the trenches. With the help of Harry Hess and dozens of other dedicated Earth scientists, Alfred Wegener was vindicated.

Over the next few years, with hundreds of Earth scientists working on the problem, seafloor spreading developed into the theory that is now known as "plate tectonics." Over the past thirty-five years, thousands of scientists have put their energy into refining the theory and applying it to different rock formations all over the world. Geologists now agree that mountain ranges do form when continents collide, that vast regions of valleys such as the East African Rift Valley and the Basin and Range in the Western United States form when continents begin to split apart, and that the continents have come together and split apart several times. Earthquakes, such as the one in San Francisco in 1906, occur when rocks break and slide past one another.

Like Alfred Wegener, Harry Hess was broad -minded and persistent. He contributed incredibly to understanding Earth's surface, but saw the need to go even further. He wanted to drill through Earth's crust to sample the mantle and he wanted to send a man out to sample the moon. He was interested in many aspects of science and was determined to figure out how they all fit together.

Harry Hess had one very important advantage that Alfred Wegener never had: he was well respected in the field of geology. Even if some geologists didn't think everything he wrote was correct, they thought highly of him and paid attention to what he had to say. He was president of several geological societies and won numerous awards. Hess was so well respected that he was put on many scientific advisory boards, including the Space Science Board and the Mohole project to drill through Earth's crust. He was also a reservist in the Navy for his adult whole life, spending several weeks a year working on bathymetry maps.

When Harry Hess died of a heart attack in 1969, he was in Woods Hole, Massachusetts, chairing a meeting of the Space Science Board. It was just one month after the first moon landing. Hess had fought hard to put a scientist on the moon, and he played a pivotal role in making the moon program a scientific affair. Harry Hammond Hess is buried in Arlington National Cemetery, near Washington, D.C.

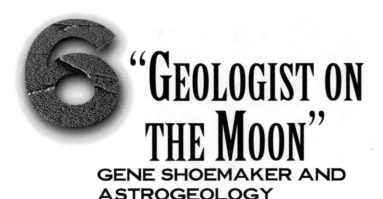

"Geologist on the Moon"

GENE SHOEMAKER AND ASTROGEOLOGY

In July 1994, Gene Shoemaker and other scientists around the world had their telescopes trained on Jupiter. They were ready for a collision no one living had ever seen before. Out in space, the U.S. spacecraft *Galileo* chanced to be in a good position to record the event, and the Hubble Space Telescope focused on the expected crash site. A comet was speeding through space, heading right for the giant planet. Although Shoemaker had long studied impact craters and had tracked the asteroids and comets that could produce them, he had never seen an actual collision before. No one had. Collisions like this generally don't occur more than once every two thousand years. Moreover, scientists had never before had the technological ability to predict or record such an event.

A little over a year before, in March 1993, Shoemaker, his wife Carolyn, and astronomer David Levy had discovered a new comet, Periodic Comet Shoemaker-Levy 9. (The 9 means it was the ninth one they had discovered.) Comets are like dirty snowballs; speeding hunks of cosmic dust and ice. This particular comet looked "squashed" when they first noticed it in photographs of the night sky. Instead of having a single head or nucleus, this comet consisted

Gene Shoemaker (1928–1997)

of at least twenty-one separate nuclei streaming along, one behind the other, through space.

A few months later, astronomers had calculated its path well enough to know that the comet might be on a collision course with Jupiter. By November, they were sure. That left half a year to plan observations. Shoemaker summed up the feeling of excitement the comet created: "Now what are the odds that this would happen in our lifetimes—with Hubble fixed, Galileo nearing Jupiter, infrared detectors having come of age, and before the money has run out? Folks, I think we've been privileged to witness a bloody miracle!"

On July 16, 1994, the first of Shoemaker-Levy's nuclei slammed into Jupiter. The force of the impact was more powerful and more spectacular than the Shoemakers or anyone else had imagined. Collisions kept coming for the next six days, as one by one, twenty-one nuclei up to three km (two miles) in diameter smashed into the

David Levy and Gene and Carolyn Shoemaker hold a drawing that depicts Comet Shoemaker-Levy 9 colliding with the planet Jupiter.

solar system's largest planet. Hot bubbles of Jovian atmosphere and cometary debris sprayed up thousands of kilometers above the clouds. For weeks, Jupiter was marked by dark scars several times the diameter of the earth.

Shoemaker's work had convinced him that sudden asteroid impacts had played an important role in geological history. However, many geologists downplayed the effects of asteroid impacts. After all, they were sudden, infrequent, catastrophic events, not the gradual, continual processes of uniformitarian geology. The crashing end of Comet Shoemaker-Levy 9 demonstrated that one sudden catastrophic event can have far-reaching effects.

THE YOUNG EUGENE M. SHOEMAKER

Eugene Merle Shoemaker was born on April 28, 1928 in Los Angeles, California. His mother was a teacher; his father took various jobs to support the family. In 1935, at the height of the Depression, his mother was offered a teaching position at Buffalo State Teachers

College in Buffalo, New York. Jobs were scarce, so she accepted, moving to Buffalo with Gene, while his father took a job for the Civilian Conservation Corps out in Wyoming.

That year, when he was seven, his mother gave Gene a gift that made a lasting impression on him. It was a set of marbles made, not of glass, but of natural stone. A fascination with beautiful polished stone stayed with Shoemaker for life. The Buffalo area also turned out to be a good place to nourish his interest in geology, because rock formations in the area are chock-full of fossils. When Gene was eight years old, his father took him to the Back Hills of South Dakota, where he began collecting rocks.

By 1942, when his family moved back out to Los Angeles, Gene Shoemaker was hooked on geology. As a student at Fairfax, then the best high school in Los Angeles, he played violin and joined the gymnastics team. During the summers, he worked for a lapidary, cutting and polishing stones. Shoemaker accelerated through high school, graduating at the age of sixteen. His parents sent him on to college at California Institute of Technology (Caltech) where he finished his Bachelor's degree in less than three years and went on for a master's. For his master's thesis, he studied some very ancient metamorphic rocks in New Mexico. By the time he was twenty years old, he had finished his degree and landed a job with the U.S. Geological Survey (USGS).

Shoemaker started with the USGS in 1948, just after World War II ended with the explosion of the first atomic bombs on Hiroshima and Nagasaki, Japan. The United States and the Soviet Union were locked in a power struggle called the Cold War. Each nation raced to develop and stockpile enough nuclear weapons to feel secure against the other's threats.

The USGS sent Shoemaker to scour the West for the uranium ore needed to fuel nuclear reactions. As Shoemaker drove around checking mining sites for uranium, it occurred to him that the Cold War rivals would soon be racing to land on the moon. Shoemaker immediately knew that he was the man for this job, "The Moon is made of rock, so geologists are the logical ones to go there . . . me, for example!" From this point on, Shoemaker set his sights on becoming the first geologist to land on the moon. He accepted any project that would help him learn more about the moon.

The year 1951 was an important one for Shoemaker. He began working on his Ph.D. at Princeton University in New Jersey; he married Carolyn Spellman, his college roommate's sister; and he went back into the field that summer to study a particular kind of uranium deposit for the USGS. These uranium deposits were in the necks of old volcanoes in Hopi Buttes, Arizona. The surrounding craters showed that these volcanoes had exploded with terrific force; in fact, they resembled some of the craters visible on the moon. Many scientists believed that the moon's craters were volcanic.

SHOEMAKER MAPS IMPACT CRATERS

As summer ended, Shoemaker stayed on to keep working on this project. In 1952 he and Carolyn drove out to Coon Butte, Arizona, to investigate Barringer Crater. This crater is a steep hole, 170 meters (560 feet) deep and twelve hundred meters (4,000 feet) across, surrounded by a rim that stands fifty meters (150 feet) above the surrounding plains.

Barringer Crater was also known as Meteor Crater because of all the meteorites scattered around it. Most geologists believed this crater was a maar crater, like those of Hopi Buttes. Maar craters form when hot magma comes into contact with groundwater. The water heats up and expands very quickly, causing an explosion of the earth above. It was a reasonable interpretation considering the crater's form and the fact that there were a lot of other maar craters in the area.

The original owner of the land, Daniel M. Barringer, disagreed with this idea. He believed that part of a crashing asteroid, not a steam explosion, had formed the crater, and some respected astronomers agreed with him. In fact, the Barringer family had spent half a million dollars digging up the crater floor, looking for the metallic remains of the asteroid. They never found it. Meanwhile, the Barringers had placed a fence around the crater and were charging admission for people to see it. On this particular day, the Shoemakers had just enough money either to eat dinner or to tour the crater. They decided to view the crater from afar.

In the 1890s, G.K. Gilbert had thought Coon Butte was an impact crater, but he could never prove it to himself or anyone else. Shoemaker also felt that it was an impact crater, but he didn't know how to prove it either until the USGS sent him to study the results of underground uranium explosions in 1956. Out in Yucca Flat, Nevada, the U.S. government was exploding uranium in underground salt deposits to see whether these explosions would create a usable form of plutonium. Shoemaker was to study the effects. What he found were craters full of rocks melted by the shock of the explosions. These craters reminded him of Barringer Crater.

Shoemaker analyzed a hunk of the glassy rock from the bottom of Barringer Crater. The rock turned out to be melted sandstone, which meant that the rock had to have been heated to over 1,500°C (2,700°F). This temperature would have to have been hotter than any lava flow. This heat must have come from an impact explosion. Shoemaker realized that the meteorite itself would not have dug a crater like Barringer. After all, meteorites are much smaller than their craters. Meteorites don't just plough into the ground; because of their great speed, they explode on impact, with enough force to melt rock and create huge holes in the ground. (If Gilbert and Barringer had known this, they wouldn't have been so disappointed that they never found a giant meteorite in the crater.)

Shoemaker's careful mapping of the crater also convinced him it must have been formed by an impact. First of all, there was no fresh volcanic rock in or around it. There were, however, the melted rock and a thick layer of broken rock on the floor. Then, when he mapped the inside wall of the crater and then the rim of the crater, he noticed that the sediments were in reverse order. On the wall, red sandstone lay on top of limestone, but on the rim, the sandstone was beneath the limestone. The rim rocks had been overturned. In places, he could even see them folded back. Shoemaker wrote up his work on Meteor Crater as a doctoral dissertation, sent it to Harry Hess at Princeton, and received his Ph.D. in 1959.

Since the early 1800s, scientists had accepted the idea that rocks fall from space, but they were still unwilling to believe that they could cause such damage. The idea was just too catastrophic. It wasn't until 1960, when another piece of evidence turned up, that geologists generally accepted the idea. Ed Chao, a scientist at the Smithsonian, found that the Barringer crater also had deposits of coesite, a mineral that forms only under extremely high pressure, like the pressure generated by a meteorite impact. The story of Barringer Crater was now complete: some 50,000 years ago an asteroid about fifty meters (150 feet) across had slammed into Earth at 65,000 kilometers (40,000 miles) per hour. In only five seconds, with the force of 20 million tons of TNT, it sent layers of rock into the air, melted the rocks it hit, turned quartz into coesite, and blasted a hole in the ground twenty times its size.

While he was working on his dissertation, Shoemaker realized that he didn't know of other impact craters to compare with this one. On Earth, water erodes craters away. On the other hand, the moon is covered in craters. At the time, most scientists thought lunar craters were volcanic, but Shoemaker wasn't so sure. He was more inclined to agree with G. K. Gilbert, Alfred Wegener, and the great astronomer Ralph B. Baldwin, who had each come to the conclusion that lunar craters formed by impact. He went to the director of the USGS to propose making a geologic map of the moon, and then started mapping the region around the crater Copernicus with a forty-year old photograph he found in a bookstore. Shoemaker studied photographs of the moon's surface to determine how its surface had evolved. He applied the same geological principles he had often applied on Earth: the law of superposition and the law of cross-cutting relations.

The law of superposition simply states that younger layers of rock form on top of older layers. Unless the formation has been turned upside down, the oldest layers in it will be those on the bottom; the layers that formed most recently will be on the top. For instance, if you see a crater that lies on top of a light-colored formation, but is partly covered over by dark material, then you can determine the order of events. First, the light-colored rocks were laid down; then, the crater formed; finally, the dark material began to fill in on top. The light material was oldest; the dark material youngest. A crater superposed on the dark material would be even younger.

The law of cross-cutting relations is similar. It says that any feature that cuts across another must be younger, more recent. For example, if a channel cuts through a rock formation, the rock formation was there first. (James Hutton had used this principle to show that granite veins must be younger than the rocks they cut through; therefore granite can't be the oldest rock on Earth.)

From the photographs, Shoemaker could distinguish three types of terrain on the moon (in fact, all three are easily visible from Earth, even without binoculars). The *lunar highlands* are light-colored, high, rough, and pocked with craters. The *maria* (Latin for "seas") are low, smooth, and dark-colored. Finally, there are the craters themselves.

In many ways, the craters were most important. Shoemaker took everything he knew about every sort of crater on Earth to determine how lunar craters formed. After studying them carefully, he concluded that most formed by meteorite impact. He then went on to show how fragments ejected from Copernicus had created fields of secondary impact craters.

Of course, Shoemaker was not the first to come to this conclusion about large craters on the moon. After comparing lunar craters to similar-looking craters all over Earth, Ralph Baldwin wrote in his 1949 book, *The Face of the Moon*, "It is concluded that the craters of the Moon have exactly the right shapes and distribution to be explained as explosion pits and that the only known source of energy great enough to produce the observed results is that carried by great meteorites." Although many astronomers agreed with Baldwin, geologists were less inclined to accept the impact theory and it was important that a *geologist* such as Shoemaker championed the cause.

Because the dark maria overlap the highlands, Shoemaker and another USGS geologist, Robert Hackman, figured this terrain formed later than the highlands. They also noticed that the maria have generally fewer craters than the highlands. This was another sign that they formed later; the maria simply haven't been there long enough to be hit by as many meteorites as the highlands have. The very youngest major feature he could find on the moon's surface was the Crater Tycho. This entire huge crater lies at the very surface; no formation overlaps it and none has filled it in. Analyses made from lunar samples show that it is only about one hundred million years old, young by lunar standards.

In fact, the number of craters in a given area was a useful index to the age of that rock: the more craters there are, the older the formation. Shoemaker and Hackman worked out the rate at which craters formed on the moon over time. They made a timeline correlating the age of a formation with the numbers and sizes of craters superimposed on it. Using this timeline, they and their colleagues could figure out the relative age of almost any formation, finish their maps, and eventually unravel the geological history of the moon.

Gene Shoemaker was particularly suited to map the moon because of all the field experience he had on Earth. He identified lunar features by comparing them to similar landforms on Earth. In many cases, there was no need to think up new ways to create a landform. He instituted a sort of variation on uniformitarianism that is now second nature to every planetary geologist: the present is the key to the past, and each planet is a key to all the others.

Shoemaker's study of impact craters on the lunar surface pioneered new scientific studies, which called *astrogeology*. His pioneering project paved the way for mapping other bodies in the solar system. Using photographs or other types of images, such as radar images of Venus, and by using impact craters to date landscapes in the same way that other geologists use fossils, scientists have since made hundreds of geological maps to decipher the histories of the other planets and their moons.

SHOEMAKER AIDS THE SPACE PROGRAM

By the time Shoemaker finished his dissertation, the Cold War had taken a new direction. Beginning with the Soviet Union's launch of *Sputnik* in 1957, the superpowers were rivals in a space race. Just as Shoemaker had guessed, it was a race to the moon. In 1959 the Soviet Union's *Luna 2*, the first spacecraft to reach the moon, crashed on the lunar surface. That same year, the Jet Propulsion Laboratory (JPL) at Caltech invited Shoemaker to join the Ranger Project. Their goal was to send a spacecraft full of scientific instruments to study the moon. Shoemaker was assigned to the TV team. This team's project was to design a television camera that could send back pictures of the moon's surface right up to the moment when the spacecraft crashed into it.

Shoemaker was thrilled. All of his projects were preparing him to realize his life's dream of actually going to the moon himself. He had been working toward this goal for fifteen years. Then, in 1963, he discovered that he had Addison's disease, a chronic illness caused by a malfunction of the adrenal gland. Addison's disease can cause blackouts, but it did not affect Shoemaker's phenomenal energy and stamina. Few people could keep up with him out in the field. Fewer could have completed the amount of work he tackled in his career. But because of this disease, Shoemaker would never be an astronaut; he would never even be allowed to get a pilot's license. He said, "Not going to the moon and banging on it with my own hammer has been the biggest disappointment in my life."

This disappointment did not keep Shoemaker from working with the space program any way he could. Early on he understood that without someone pushing hard for science, the space program was in danger of just being an event for politicians and the media.

Most bureaucrats and engineers of the National Aeronautics and Space Administration (NASA) couldn't care less about understanding the moon. Shoemaker knew that the Cold War space race was a chance, maybe the only chance, to gather the detailed photographs and samples that scientists needed to understand the moon. His skillful lobbying and proven scientific expertise convinced NASA to accept science into the lunar program.

In 1961 the first Ranger spacecraft failed. So did the next five. In some, the instruments failed; two missed the moon altogether. Finally, in 1964, *Ranger* 7 made it to the moon and sent back the first close up view of the lunar surface before it crashed. Then, in 1965, *Rangers* 8 and 9 succeeded in sending back thousands of additional photographs. The next goal was to create a spacecraft that could make a soft landing—the *Surveyor*. Shoemaker signed on for this project, too.

One of the problems bothering both scientists and engineers was that they weren't certain what the surface of the moon was like. Was the surface solid rock, soft sediment, or meters and meters of loose dust that would swallow a manned lander? If it was solid rock, was it basalt? Was it volcanic tuff from explosive volcanoes? Or was it something entirely different?

In May 1966, on the very first try, *Surveyor 1* landed softly on the moon's surface and sent back thousands of images. Five more *Surveyor* missions enabled Shoemaker to observe in detail the fragmental material that constitutes the uppermost layers of the moon. He called it the "lunar regolith." Surveyor's instruments also confirmed what many (including Baldwin and Shoemaker) already thought: that under this regolith, the dark maria were made of solid basalt. In January 1968, *Surveyor 7* soft-landed right on the rim of the Crater Tycho in a field of boulders. The information it transmitted enabled Shoemaker to figure out what kind of rock the meteorite that formed Tycho had smashed into (*anorthositic gabbro*). Later analyses of lunar rocks collected from the highlands by the Apollo astronauts proved him right.

Harry Hess also knew how important the space program was to geology. In 1964, he was in charge of the search committee for scientist-astronauts, but then went off to Cambridge for the year. Hess decided that Shoemaker was the best man to fill the position. With their detailed knowledge of the moon's surface, Shoemaker and the geologists he hired were able to suggest safe and interesting landing spots for the Apollo missions. Then, as the Apollo program's primary investigator for field geology, he made sure that geology fieldwork was part of the scientific agenda of the moon landings. Shoemaker and the geology teams taught the astronauts how to identify rocks and minerals, taught them the sorts of observations to make, and took them on field trips to practice.

All this practice paid off when *Apollo 11* landed on the moon in July 1969. During their moonwalks, astronauts Neil Armstrong and Edwin (Buzz) Aldrin collected twenty-two kg (50 lbs. on Earth) of

Edwin Aldrin, an astronaut on the Apollo 11 lunar landing mission, poses beside the U.S. flag planted on the Moon.

lunar rocks; set up a seismometer to measure impact vibrations; and made observations of the terrain around them. After five more successful landings, geologists had learned without a doubt what the lunar surface is like (rock-strewn and dusty), what the maria are made of (basalt), what the highlands are made of (anorthosite and related rocks), and how old the rocks are (the samples ranged from 100 million to 4,500 million years old).

Besides collecting rocks from the Moon's surface, Aldrin took samples from the lunar soil. Here, he drives a tube into the soil to extract a sample.

SHOEMAKER STUDIES ASTEROIDS
AND COMETS

By the time the Apollo program was coming to an end in the early 1970s, Shoemaker had already started another project. His many years of studying craters got him interested in the bodies that formed the craters: asteroids and comets. After seeing the tremendous damage that impacts could cause, he began to wonder about the risk of just such an impact on Earth. Measuring the rate of impact on the moon is possible because the moon's surface is not affected by water and weather as Earth's is. The constant process of erosion made it impossible to figure out a similar rate for Earth. Shoemaker turned to the sky for an answer.

With fellow scientist Eleanor Helin, he used the oldest telescope in the Palomar Observatory in southern California to survey the night sky for asteroids and comets. They were looking for asteroids or comets whose orbits could intersect Earth's orbit. If the orbits crossed each other, there was a possibility that at some time in the future, the body and the planet could collide. It was a tedious process. After taking photographs at forty-five minute intervals, they would use a stereoscope to look at two images at once. Stationary objects would be clear dots. Moving objects would look fuzzy and seem to float in 3-D above the background. By the end of the 1970s, Shoemaker and Helin had doubled the number of known asteroids whose orbits crossed Earth's path.

In 1982 Shoemaker's wife Carolyn joined the asteroid-watching team. For years she had been occupied raising their three children. Once the children were grown, Carolyn Shoemaker found that she had a knack for spotting possible comets and asteroids. She was the first to spot Periodic Comet Shoemaker-Levy 9. Right now, she holds the all-time, world record for discovering comets. Because of their discovery of Shoemaker-Levy 9, the scientific world was prepared to study this comet's spectacular collision with Jupiter.

From a lifetime of study of the craters on Earth and the comets and asteroids in the sky, Shoemaker was able to project an asteroid collision timeline for Earth. He calculated that a four meter (thirteen foot) meteorite might fall on Earth once a year (although there is a seventy percent chance it will fall into an ocean). Once every one hundred years, Earth might be hit by a meteorite twenty meters (66 feet) across. And once every 100,000,000 years Earth might be clobbered by a meteorite ninety km (56 miles) across. It was a meteorite this size that slammed into the Yucatan Peninsula 65 million years ago, an event that scientists think may have caused the extinction of the dinosaurs. Shoemaker helped show that meteorite impact is a significant geological process that has shaped Earth. Early in its history, Earth was bombarded constantly. After all, it formed from the accumulation of smaller bodies in the first place, and to a small degree, it is still accumulating. Impacts may seen "catastrophic" to us, but to Earth, they are just growing pains.

To figure out the rates of impact, Shoemaker not only studied the skies but also traveled the globe to inspect possible impact craters. Ever since his early days working for the USGS, he had been on the alert to identify impact craters on Earth. Although he had seen thousands of images of craters on the moon, it was still thrilling to find a crater he could walk around in. Not every crater is formed by meteorite impact; some are caused by volcanism. Shoemaker became an authority on identifying which ones actually were impact craters. He looked for melted rocks, overturned sediment layers, broken rock in the crater bottom, and high-pressure "shock" minerals.

Geologists now know of about 160 impact craters on Earth. Shoemaker identified many of them in Texas and Iowa; in Germany, Saudi Arabia, and Russia; and especially, in Australia. Australia is an excellent place to look for impact craters. The center of the Australian continent is composed of ancient rock that has not been split or folded by the movement of tectonic plates for hundreds of millions of years. In addition, the climate of central Australia is very dry. Rivers are few and erosion is very slow. Surface features in Australia last for a long time. For all these reasons, Australia has the most complete record of impact craters on Earth.

SHOEMAKER'S LEGACY

The Shoemakers got into the habit of making a yearly summer trip to Australia to search for impact craters. They were in central Australia on July 18, 1997, when Gene Shoemaker was killed in a head-on collision on a rough, gravel road. He was sixty-nine years old. Carolyn Shoemaker survived the crash, but she and scientists around the world had suffered a great loss.

Everyone who had known Shoemaker knew that going to the moon had been his life's dream. When one of his former students learned of his death, she decided to try to arrange for Shoemaker to make it to the moon. The former student, Carolyn Porco, was now a planetary scientist at the Lunar and Planetary Lab of the University of Arizona. She knew that a spacecraft called the *Lunar Prospector* was due to be launched that winter. The *Prospector* would orbit the moon collecting images and then end its mission by crashing into it. She petitioned NASA to send some of Shoemaker's ashes up on the *Prospector*.

The petition caused controversy. Some people feared it would set a bad precedent and that NASA would be bombarded by requests to be buried on the moon. The Navajo Nation objected to putting human remains on the moon. Other people complained about the cost, although it was all paid for privately.

On the other hand, everyone who had a hand in the space program knew what Shoemaker had accomplished. He had insisted that the U.S. space program take advantage of its unprecedented chance to do scientific research. He had inspired the tremendous development of planetary geology during his lifetime. Moreover, he had not let his personal disappointment about going to the moon sour him on teaching others what to do when they got there. His vision and enthusiasm made planetary geology a routine part of the U.S. space program and the U.S. Geological Survey.

The decision whether or not to send Shoemaker's ashes to the moon came to the desk of Wes Huntress, NASA Associate Administrator for Space Science. He decided, "For this particular man, this was the right thing to do."

On January 6, 1998, the *Lunar Prospector* took off from Cape Canaveral, Florida. Among all the instruments aboard was a capsule containing one ounce of Gene Shoemaker's ashes. Eighteen and a half months later, on July 31, 1999, the *Prospector* crashed into the south pole of the moon. Carolyn Shoemaker expressed the family's gratitude: "This is so important to us. . . .We will always know when we look at the moon, that Gene is there."

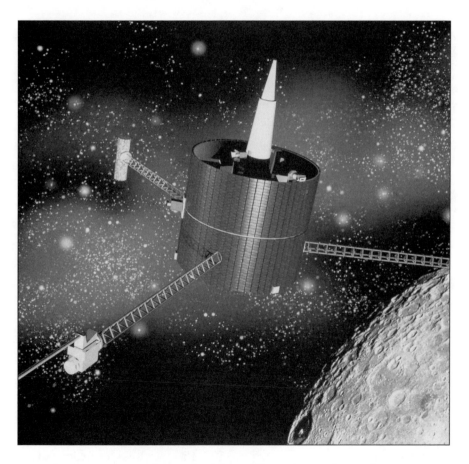

The Lunar Prospector *carried Gene Shoemaker's ashes to the Moon.*

APPENDIX 1
GEOLOGIC TIME SCALE

ERA	PERIOD	EPOCH	MILLION YEARS AGO	EVENTS
Archean	pre-Cambrian		4560-2500	solar system forms; life begins to evolve
Proterozoic			2500-570	life evolves to more complex forms; the atmosphere becomes oxygen-rich
Paleozoic	Cambrian		570-505	first limestone reefs
	Ordovician		505-438	rocks at Glen Tilt form; Appalachians begin to form
	Silurian		438-408	Siccar Point grey schist forms
	Devonian		408-360	Siccar Point red sandstone is deposited
	Carboniferous (Mississipian) (Pennsylvanian)		360-245	widespread coal swamps
	Permian		286-245	Mesosaurs inhabit Pangaea

ERA	PERIOD	EPOCH	MILLION YEARS AGO	EVENTS
Mesozoic	Triassic		245-208	Pangaea begins to rift apart
	Jurassic		208-144	Atlantic Ocean basin begins to form
	Cretaceous		144-65	first flowering plants; Tycho— youngest major feature of the Moon forms
Cretaceous/ Tertiary boundary			65	Large impactor strikes the Yucatan; dinosaurs die out
Cenozoic	Tertiary	Paleocene	65-58	
		Eocene	58-37	Alps begin to form (stop forming in the late Miocene)
		Oligocene	37-24	igneous rocks of the Henry Mountains intrude
		Miocene	24-5	Colorado Plateau begins to uplift: Henry Mountains begin to form; Grand Canyon begins to form; Himalayas begin to form (are still forming)
		Pliocene	5-1.8	
	Quaternary	Pleistocene	1.8 million- 10,000 years ago	Meteor Crater forms; Lake Bonneville exists; Ice Ages; Megatherium lives
		Holocene	10,000 years ago-today	1906 San Francisco earthquake

APPENDIX 2
THE AGE AND STRUCTURE OF EARTH

THE AGE OF EARTH

The sun, Earth, and the rest of the planets in our solar system formed about 4.56 billion years ago. Scientists know this from analyzing meteorites that formed at the same time and haven't changed composition since. Earth's crust is a bit younger: the oldest rock found so far is a gneiss discovered in Canada. This rock is about 3.9 billion years old.

THE STRUCTURE OF EARTH

Earth can be divided into four parts: crust, mantle, outer core, and inner core. The crust is the outer shell, the part we live on. There are two types of crust: continental and oceanic. Continental crust is on average about thirty-five km (22 miles) thick, but it is much thicker under mountain chains and thinner under low valleys and plains. It is composed of igneous, sedimentary, and metamorphic rocks that range in age from zero to almost four billion years old. The oceanic crust is thin (only about seven km [4 miles]) and is composed of the igneous rocks, basalt and gabbro, with a covering of sediment. It is denser than the continental crust. The oldest oceanic crust is only about 180 million years old.

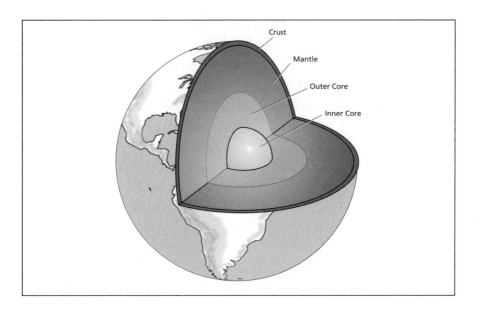

The interior of Earth is divided into four layers. The crust is the thinnest layer. Next, the mantle is a thick layer of solid rock about 1,800 miles (2,900 km) thick. The outer core is about 1,400 miles (2,250 km) thick and composed of liquid iron and nickel. Inside this is the inner core. This area is about the size of the Moon. It is composed of solid iron and nickel.

Below the crust is the mantle. It is dense and hot and is composed of rocks rich in iron and magnesium minerals. Because it is under pressure from the crust above, the mantle is solid rock. In places, some of it melts, forming magma that will eventually solidify into the igneous rock basalt.

Below the mantle is Earth's core. The core is very dense and is probably composed of iron and nickel. The outer core is not solid, but a liquid, or liquid-crystal mush. The inner core is hotter, but because it is under even more pressure, it is solid. Most of what we know about the interior of Earth comes from analyzing seismic waves.

PLATE TECTONICS

Earth's surface is mobile. It is divided into "plates" that are composed of the brittle crust and uppermost mantle. These plates ride on the mantle below, which moves slowly. In some places, the plates collide; in some places, they diverge; in others, they slide past one another. It is these motions that have resulted in the overall form of Earth's surface.

Mountain chains form when two continents collide. Deep submarine trenches form when an ocean plate collides with another plate and dives beneath it. Continental rift valleys, such as the East African rift, form as contents begin to split. Mid-ocean ridges form where two ocean plates are separating, causing magma to well up from the mantle, creating a volcanic mountain range. Large strike-slip faults, like the San Andreas, are boundaries where two plates slide past one another.

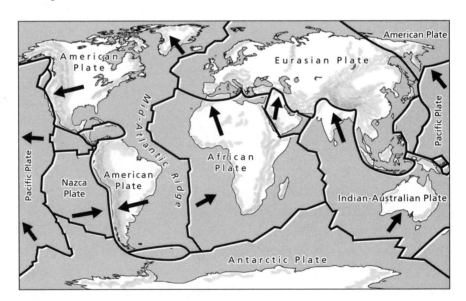

GLOSSARY

anorthositic gabbro–a light-colored plutonic igneous rock; makes up the lunar highlands

asteroid–a small rocky body that orbits the sun; common in a region between Mars and Jupiter called the Asteroid Belt

basalt–a dark-colored volcanic rock. Basaltic lava is fluid and very hot. It erupts from the mid-ocean ridges, from oceanic islands, from some volcanoes on the continents, and also makes up the lunar maria

calcium carbonate–$CaCO_3$; the chemical compound that makes up the mineral calcite and the rocks limestone, chalk, and marble

catastrophism–the philosophy that Earth's form is a result of a single, or a few major, world-wide catastrophes and that the processes acting on Earth today are insignificant in shaping it

chalk–fine grained limestone made from the skeletons of tiny sea animals called coccoliths

coal–a metamorphosed sedimentary rock composed of ancient swamp plants

comet–a mass of dust and ice orbiting the sun

conglomerate–a sedimentary rock made up of rounded pieces of other rocks, held together with a natural cement; many conglomerates began as piles of pebbles on a beach or in a streambed

contact–the surface between two different rock formations

continental crust–the part of Earth's crust that makes up the continents and continental shelves

continental drift–the theory that the continents move slowly over Earth's surface

convection–movement of material (e.g., air, water, or rock) in a circular pattern as a result of the differences in density throughout the material: dense material sinks and light material rises.

crater–a semi-spherical hole in the ground; some craters are formed by volcanic explosions, some are formed by meteorite impacts

crop rotation–the agricultural practice of growing a different crop on a particular piece of farmland each year in order to replenish the nutrients in the soil

crust–the thin, rocky, outer shell of the earth; there are two types of crust: continental crust and oceanic crust

delta–a deposit of mud and sand that forms where a river meets the sea; from above, deltas are shaped like the Greek letter delta

density–mass per unit of volume; if there are two materials of the same volume, the one that is more massive (and therefore weighs more), is denser

deposit–(v) to lay down; (n) an accumulation of rocks or mineral grains (e.g., a gravel deposit); (n) a concentration of a mineable mineral (e.g., a copper deposit)

dike–a sheet-shaped formation of igneous rock that has intruded another rock

diluvialism–the philosophy that the Deluge, or Biblical Flood, shaped Earth's surface and deposited most rocks

Enlightenment–the philosophical movement of the seventeenth and eighteenth centuries that emphasized reasoning as the way to understand the world; also known as the Age of Reason

erosion–the breaking down and wearing away of rocks and landscapes through the action of forces such as water, wind, and gravity

erratic–a rock that has been eroded from its original location and deposited somewhere else by a glacier

extrusive rock–volcanic rock

fault–(n) a break in a rock formation; a plane along which rocks move past one another, or have moved past each other; there are three types of faults: normal faults, reverse (or thrust) faults, and strike-slip faults. Along a *normal fault*, the block above the fault moves down with respect to the block below the fault. Along a *reverse fault*, the block above the fault moves up and over the block below. Along a *strike-slip fault*, the two blocks move horizontally past one another; (v) to break and move against

fault line–the line marking the intersection of a fault with Earth's surface

field geologist–a geologist who studies rocks and landscapes outside (in the field) as opposed to in the laboratory

fracture–(n) a planar break in a rock; (v) to break

geochemistry–the study of the detailed chemistry of rocks and minerals, a branch of geology

geology–the study of the Earth's structure, its history, and the processes that shape it; geology also includes the study of the structure, history, and processes that shape the other rocky planets and moons in the solar system

geomorphology–the study of landforms, a branch of geology

geophysics–a branch of geology that uses principles of physics to study the earth; geophysicists study things like gravity, magnetics, electrical properties, and seismic waves

glacier–a mass of consolidated ice that moves very slowly, like a river; glaciers are metamorphic rocks primarily composed of the mineral ice

granite–a white, grey, pink, or red, coarse-grained, plutonic igneous rock; granite is the main component of the continental crust

gravity–a force of attraction between two bodies; the force of gravity depends on the masses of the two objects and the distance from each other: the more massive the objects, and the closer they are to each other, the greater the force of gravity

guyot–a flat-topped, underwater mountain; most are old volcanoes

hydraulic mining–a type of mining using very powerful jets of water to wash away soft rock formations containing useful minerals; much gold was extracted from the American West by hydraulic mining

igneous intrusion–a rock formation made of igneous rock that has invaded another rock and solidified within it; dikes and laccoliths are both igneous intrusions

igneous rock–a rock that has solidified from molten rock, or magma. There are two types of igneous rock: volcanic (or extrusive) and plutonic (or intrusive).

impactor–an object (for instance, a meteorite, asteroid, or comet) that hits a planetary surface

intrusive rock–plutonic rock

isostasy–the condition of gravitational equilibrium of Earth's crust; it is similar to floating: heavy regions sink, light regions float higher

laccolith–a lens-shaped igneous intrusion with a flat floor and a convex roof

lava–molten rock on Earth's surface

limestone–a sedimentary rock composed of the mineral calcite; most limestone forms from the accumulation of skeletons and shells of small marine creatures, and the precipitation of calcite from seawater

magma–molten rock, or a crystal and liquid mush, that solidifies to form igneous rocks; if it is on Earth's surface it is called lava

mantle–the layer of hot, dense, solid rock beneath the crust

maria–the smooth, dark plains on the moon

marl–a soft grey sediment composed of clay and calcium carbonate

metamorphic rock–a rock that has been changed from its original form by heat, pressure, or both (e.g., when buried, the sedimentary rock limestone turns into, or metamorphoses, into the metamorphic rock marble)

meteor–a piece of rock from outer space that burns up while travelling through Earth's atmosphere; also known as a shooting star

meteorite–a rock of any size that has traveled from outer space, through Earth's atmosphere, and hit Earth's surface

mid-ocean ridge, or mid-ocean rift–a 60,000-km long volcanic mountain range that winds around Earth on the seafloor; the ridges are also rifts where the oceanic crust is being torn apart

mineralogy–the study of minerals, a branch of geology

Neptunists–a group of natural philosophers of the eighteenth and nineteenth centuries who believed that most rocks, including granite and basalt, had been deposited from a primeval sea

oceanic crust–the thin crust that underlies the oceans

petrology–a branch of geology that involves the study of rocks, their composition, and how they form

plate tectonics–the theory that Earth's crust and uppermost mantle are separated into a number of pieces, or plates, that move over the Earth, riding on the convecting mantle below; plate tectonics explains the origins of mountain chains, submarine volcanic ridges, submarine trenches, large faults, and the locations and origins of some earthquakes and volcanoes

plutonic rock–an igneous rock that has solidified below Earth's surface, also known as an intrusive rock; granite is a plutonic rock

Plutonists–a group of natural philosophers of the late eighteenth and early nineteenth centuries who thought that rocks such as granite and basalt solidified from hot, molten rock

precipitate–(v) the process of ions (charged atoms) in a fluid combining to form a solid; for instance, sodium and chlorine ions in water combine to precipitate salt; (n) a mineral or rock formed in this way; salt is a precipitate

rift–a valley caused by extension and faulting of Earth's crust

sal ammoniac–the chemical compound NH_4Cl, also known as ammonium chloride

sandstone–a sedimentary rock composed of small grains of sand cemented together naturally

scarp–a straight cliff or steep slope-face created by erosion or faulting

schist–a layered metamorphic rock, similar to slate, that forms when sediments are metamorphosed through burial and heating

seamount–a submarine mountain

sedimentary rock–a rock composed of pieces of smaller rocks and mineral grains that have been eroded from another rock and then naturally cemented together (e.g., sandstone, conglomerate); a rock formed through the precipitation of minerals from water (e.g. salt, limestone); sedimentary rocks commonly form layers, or beds; a rock composed of organic matter, such as plants or shells

strata–layers or beds of rock

stratigraphic map–a map indicating the types of strata, or rock formations, that are exposed at the surface or shallowly buried beneath soil, vegetation, and buildings in a particular area; a type of geological map

stratigraphy–the study of the layers, or strata, of rocks and what they indicate about Earth's history

tectonics–the processes that deform Earth's surface and form broad structures such as mountain chains; (note: not all tectonics is "plate tectonics")

trench–a long, relatively narrow valley on the seafloor

unconformity–a contact between two rock formations in which one formation formed much later than the other, or under very different environmental conditions; a gap in the geological record (as a result of erosion or a halt in deposition); (e.g., the contact between an Archean metamorphic rock and a Mesozoic sedimentary rock; or the contact between a body of granite and the limestone it has intruded)

uniformitarianism–the principle specifying that the processes responsible for the formation and shape of Earth in the past are the same processes acting on it today; a method of interpreting how rocks and landscapes formed in the past by studying the processes that form and shape them today

vein–a thin filling of rock in a fracture

volcanic rock–a rock formed when liquid rock (magma) solidifies on Earth's surface; basalt is a volcanic rock

weathering–the changing of rocks and minerals through the action of water, air, and biological activity. Minerals weather to form new minerals. For instance, rusting is a type of weathering in which iron mixes with the oxygen in air and water to form iron-oxide: rust

BIBLIOGRAPHY AND INTERNET RESOURCES

Both geology and history are very broad subjects. We have attempted to explain some basic principles of geology, but there are many concepts that we've had to gloss over (most notably regarding plate tectonics), and many more that we haven't mentioned at all. The following is a list of books and Web sites that were helpful to us in writing this book, and that we hope you will find useful as well. (Remember that our detailed understanding of Earth and the other planets changes all the time. More recent science books are generally more reliable than older ones.)

GENERAL

Adams, Frank Dawson. *The Birth and Development of the Geological Sciences*. New York: Dover, 1990.

Faul, Henry and Carol Faul. *It Began With a Stone: a history of geology from the stone age to the age of plate tectonics*. (A Wiley-Interscience Publication). New York: John Wiley & Sons, 1983.

Fenton, Carroll Lane and Mildred Adams Fenton. *Giants of Geology*. New York: Doubleday & Co., 1952.

Gould, Stephen Jay. *Time's Arrow—Time's Cycle: myth and metaphor in the discovery of geological time*. Cambridge, MA: Harvard University Press, 1987.

U.S. Geological Survey
http://www.usgs.gov

Earth Today (Smithsonian Institution)
http://www.nasm.si.edu/earthtoday/

History of GeoSciences
http://geoclio.st.usm.edu

JAMES HUTTON

Dean, Dennis R. *James Hutton and the History of Geology*. Ithaca, NY: Cornell University Press, 1992.

Craig, G. Y. and J. H. Hull, eds. *James Hutton : present and future*. London: Geological Society of London, 1999.

Craig, G. Y., D.B. McIntyre, and C. D. Waterston. *James Hutton's Theory of the Earth: the lost drawings*. Edinburgh: Scottish Academic Press, 1978.

Hutton, James. *Theory of the Earth; or an investigation of the laws observable in the composition, dissolution, and restoration of the land upon the globe*. Transactions of the Royal Society of Edinburgh, vol. 1, pp. 209-304, 1788.

Playfair, John. *James Hutton & Joseph Black: biographies*, Transactions of the Royal Society of Edinburgh, 1805. Edinburgh: RSE Scotland Foundation, 1997.

Playfair, John. *Illustrations of the Huttonian Theory of the Earth*. Mineola, NY: Dover Publications, 1964.

Field Trip Guide to Hutton's Unconformity at Siccar Point
http://www.glg.ed.ac.uk/courses/field/siccarpt

CHARLES LYELL

Blundell, Derek J. and Andrew C. Scott, eds. *Lyell: the past is the key to the present.* London: Geological Society of London, 1998.

Bonney, T. G. *Charles Lyell and Modern Geology.* New York: Macmillan, 1895.

Lyell, Charles. *Principles of Geology.* Chicago: University of Chicago Press, 1991.

Lyell, Charles. *Life, Letters, and Journals of Sir Charles Lyell, bart. Edited by his sister-in-law, Mrs. Lyell.* London: J. Murray, 1881.

Wilson, Leonard G. *Charles Lyell, the years to 1841: the revolution in geology.* New Haven: Yale University Press, 1972.

Wilson, Leonard G. *Lyell in America: transatlantic geology, 1841–1853.* Baltimore: Johns Hopkins University Press, 1998.

G. K. GILBERT AND THE AMERICAN WEST

Bartlett, Richard. *Great Surveys of the American West.* Norman: University of Oklahoma Press, 1962.

Gilbert, Grove Karl. *Geology of the Henry Mountains, Utah, as recorded in the notebooks of G. K. Gilbert, 1875-76.* (The Geological Society of America, Memoir 167). Boulder, CO: The Geological Society of America, 1988.

Pyne, Stephen J. *Grove Karl Gilbert, a great engine of research.* Austin: University of Texas Press, 1980.

Yochelson, Ellis, ed. *The Scientific Ideas of G.K. Gilbert: an assessment on the occasion of the centennial of the U.S.G.S. (1879-1979).* Boulder, CO: Geological Society of America, 1980.

San Francisco Earthquake of 1906

http://quake.wr.usgs.gov/more/1906

History of the U.S. Geological Survey

http://www.usgs.gov/reports/circulars/

Meteor Crater
http://www.barringercrater.com

ALFRED WEGENER AND CONTINENTAL DRIFT

Marvin, Ursula. *Continental Drift—the evolution of a concept*. Washington, DC: Smithsonian Institution Press, 1973.

Schwarzbach, Martin. *Alfred Wegener: father of continental drift*. Trans. Carla Love. Madison, WI: Science Tech, 1986.

Wegener, Alfred. *The Origin of Continents and Oceans*. New York: Dover, 1962.

HARRY HESS AND PLATE TECTONICS

Glen, William. *The Road to Jaramillo: critical years of the revolution in earth science*. Stanford, CA: Stanford University Press, 1982.

Hallam, Anthony. *A Revolution in the Earth Sciences: from continental drift to plate tectonics*. Oxford: Clarendon Press, 1973.

Keary, Philip and Frederick J. Vine. *Global Tectonics*. Oxford: Blackwell Scientific Publications, 1996.

Menard, H. W. *Ocean of Truth: a personal history of global tectonics*. Princeton, NJ: Princeton University Press, 1986.

Plate Tectonics
http://pubs.usgs.gov/publications/text/dynamic.html

Paleomap Project: The earth through time
http://www.scotese.com/

Views of the Earth Today
http://www.ldeo.columbia.edu/~small/GDEM.html

GENE SHOEMAKER AND
PLANETARY GEOLOGY

Levy, David. *Quest For Comets: an explosive trail of beauty and danger.* New York: Plenum Press, 1994.

Stephens, Hal G. and Eugene M. Shoemaker. *In the Footsteps of John Wesley Powell: an album of comparative photographs of the Green and Colorado rivers, 1871-72 and 1968.* Boulder, CO: Johnson Books, 1987.

Wilhelms, Don E. *To a Rocky Moon: a geologist's history of lunar exploration.* Tuscon: The University of Arizona Press, 1993.

Wilhelms, Don. E. *The Geologic History of the Moon.* U.S. Geological Survey Professional Paper 1348. Washington, DC: U.S. Government Printing Office, 1987.

Meteor Crater

http://www.barringercrater.com

Exploring the Moon

http://cass.jsc.nasa.gov/moon.html

Comet Shoemaker-Levy 9

http://www.jpl.nasa.gov/
http://nssdc.gsfc.nasa.gov/planetary/comet.html

INDEX

ABOUT THE AUTHORS

Margaret W. Carruthers grew up in Towson, Maryland. She received a B.S. in Natural Resources from the University of the South in Sewanee, Tennessee, in 1992 and then went on to the University of Massachusetts–Amherst, where she was awarded an M.S. in Geology in 1996. For four years she worked as a geologist and educator at the American Museum of Natural History in New York City. She is now living and writing in Oxford, England, with her husband, cosmochemist Richard Ash. Margaret is also co-author of the *Audubon First Field Guide: Rocks and Minerals* (Scholastic, 1998).

Susan Maloney Clinton is a free-lance writer specializing in children's nonfiction. Her biographical and historical books have covered a variety of subjects and events ranging from Jurassic times to the present. She holds a Ph.D. in English from Northwestern University, where she taught literature courses part-time for ten years. She has contributed articles to reference works, such as *Encyclopedia Brittanica* and *Compton's Encyclopedia*, and written textbook and computer materials for several educational publishers. She is also the author of the Lives in Science book, *Reading Between the Bones: The Pioneers of Dinosaur Paleontology*. Ms. Clinton lives in New Jersey with her husband Patrick and their children.